20 Varied R
in the historic
Midland Shires

drawings by Jenny Taylor

THORNHILL PRESS
1985

ISBN 0 946328 10 2

Illustrations by Jenny Taylor

Printed by Logos Limited, Cinderford, Glos

Published by
Thornhill Press
24 Moorend Road
Cheltenham

INTRODUCTION

Our twenty selected rambles are circular and varied, each one designed for a day's walk combined with sight-seeing, and a midday break at a carefully chosen inn. They are numbered in the table of contents and again on the back cover, and should appeal equally to rambling groups, families or individuals, and can be modified to suit personal tastes. A map of each route is accompanied by a synopsis with details of the ground covered, to enable a choice to be made according to the weather, and the conditions underfoot, at any time of the year. Maps and synopses together should satisfy the purist, but for the more meditative, footnotes with local details are provided.

The scale used for the maps is 3cm = 1 kilometre
(except map 4 page 22 & map 18 page 89)

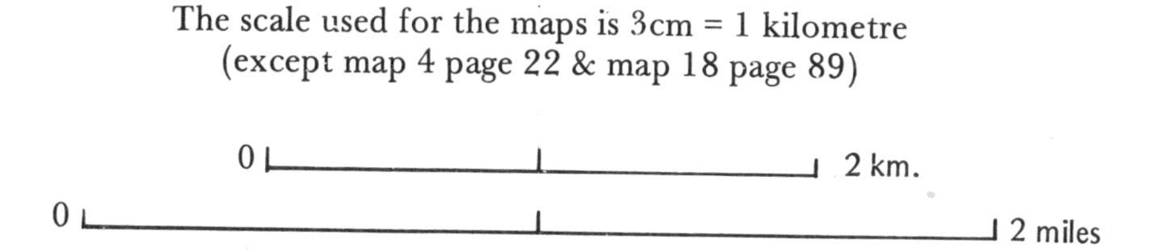

The Midland counties have been graced by nature with gentle hills and soft-flowing rivers; unspectacular perhaps, but touched by the moving hand of history. Here, in these now peaceful shires was hatched the infamous Gunpowder Plot, and after its failure, the pitiful remnants of the Catholic gentry found precarious shelter in their last strongholds. In this castle a wretched king was deposed, and at this altar another king prayed for victory in the forthcoming battle, only to lose his crown and his life that day. At Naseby the fate of Charles I was decided, and the future of parliamentary government determined.

The lives of the Midlanders were never easy or divorced from stern reality, and their history is reflected in their houses, villages and churches? some of them monuments to the wealth created by the all-consuming sheep, others memorials to the struggles of their past. Everywhere too are the signs of their agricultural post, in the medieval ridge and furrow, and the tall quickset hedgerows.

This rich heritage is fast disappearing beneath the remorseless advance of the plough. Therefore, although the maps have been drawn with the utmost care, we recommend with them the use of the O.S. 1:50,000 or better still, the 1:25,000 sheets, as the footpaths and rights of way are no longer sacred. It takes courage to walk over a waterlogged ploughed field, or through standing corn where the path has been obliterated, but it must be done if we are to retain our ancient birthright in the face of the agricultural juggernaut.

Finally, our thanks to Jenny who provided the drawings, to Max, Geoff and Brian, three gentlemen of Leamington who have been unfailingly cheerful walking companions, and to Mollie and Beryl, who kindly read through the text.

ILLUSTRATIONS

CONTENTS

WALK 1

BOSWORTH FIELD BATTLE CENTRE – MARKET BOSWORTH – SUTTON CHENEY – BATTLE CENTRE

Distance a.m. 2½ miles, p.m. 3 approx. O.S. Map No. 140 (Leicester and Coventry) 1:50,000. Start point Battle Centre car park. Grid ref. 402002.

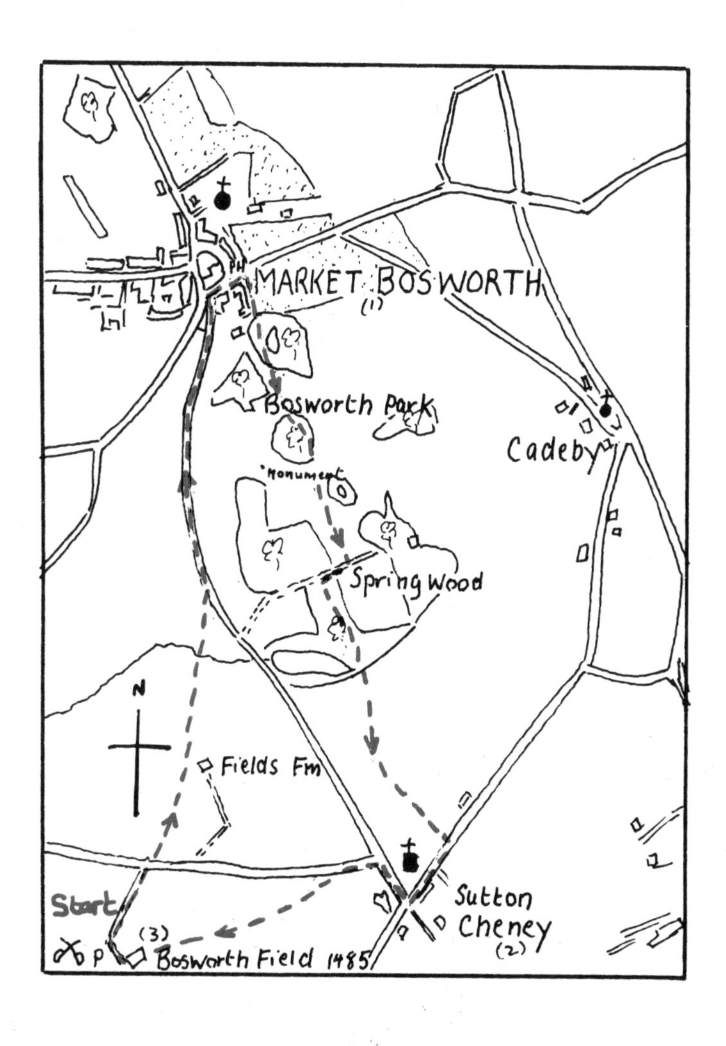

This is a delightful, easy ramble over flat, fertile Leicestershire farmland with lunch at the peaceful town of Market Bosworth (1), followed by a return walk through Bosworth Park to Sutton Cheney (2) and the fascinating Battle Centre (3), which if desired can itself form the base for a day out.

Start by taking the lane away from the Centre with King Richard's banner of the White Boar floating lazily to the left on Ambion Hill. Already the spire of Market Bosworth church signals the lunch-time objective. The way dips down under a tall ash to a road across which is a stile. A path goes diagonally across the field ahead, but if the corn is green or standing, the farmer has left room to follow the right-hand boundary up to a plastic animal shelter near the outbuildings. From here go left along the hedge and leave the grain field for a pleasant meadow. At the hedge corner go half right towards another ash beneath which is a foot-bridge of planks across the reedy stream.

Follow the stream keeping the tall hawthorn hedge on the right. Heavily-laden crab apple trees favour this hedgerow. At a gate in the right-hand corner cross the stream and turn left. The magnificent hedgerow with its autumn fruits of crab apples and sloes now overshadows the route on the left as far as a double gate and lane with wide verges. Turn left and follow this under stately oaks. On the right is Bosworth Park, with a statue standing up on the skyline amid the grain, and that great spire in the background. Soon a white gate where town and country meet leads into the quiet street and open market place of the little town, long since removed from the glare of history.

On Mondays, the 'Old Black Horse' on the right is foodless, but on other days it excels. Across the cobbles though is 'Softleys', a wine bar where food and drink is served by a very pleasant young couple.

The afternoon begins with a stroll up Rectory Lane at the end of the row of thatched houses near the 'Old Black Horse', then past the market to the park on the right where near two sycamores a sign of a white foot points right. Keep the fence on that side and go through this pleasant open space to a large fishing lake and continue along its right edge. At the lake's end a grass track goes right through a copse of silver birch and left through a wicket gate in a wooden fence under a lime tree. Follow the well-beaten track through Bosworth Park with a wood on the right. A small stone pyramid stands in the corn on the left, and on the right some distance away is the statue seen in the morning – Hercules clad in the skin of a Nemean lion, slain by him as his first labour. These were adornments in the Dixie family park, but the great beeches, chestnuts, oaks and limes are far grander memorials to them. Soon a large pool appears on the right and a gabled lodge lies ahead. Go on and skirt the wood on the left, with a wire fence on the right, come out of it on to a track by the lodge, turn right for a few yards and then left by an iron railing. Follow the farm track with the hedge on the left. The broken ground is covered with a profusion of fat hen and spangled with white mayweed. Keeping the wood on the left, come to a stream in the field corner – dog-leg left and then right and go up the corn field beneath the ashes with the hedge now on the right. Continue uphill, bend right and then left always with the hedge on the right. Primitive horsetails and colourful willow-herb abound here, and a white house on the left marks the road line. Emerge on to the road, and walk to the right past the Greyhound Inn and the Elizabethan mansion now called Hall Farm. This is Sutton Cheney and on the right is St James's church. Walk to the right past it and continue to the road junction, where go left uphill to Cheney Lane picnic site. Pass through the gate and cross the meadows, following the well-plaited hedge on the right, and so return to the Battle Centre.

(1) The peaceful little town is notable for two ancient buildings. The square stone grammar school with its rather austere facade bears a Latin inscription informing the world that it was founded in 1561 and restored in 1828 by the trustees of Wolstan Dixie, wealthy local landowner and benefactor. The young and penurious Samuel Johnson came to teach grammar here, found the place and the task distasteful, and reckoned his life was "as unvaried as the cuckoo's note", an apt description of the routine aspects of the profession.

The church of St Peter, situated in Park Street which has some attractive brick cottages, is framed by a backcloth of beeches, pines and yews. The tall spire dates from the 15th century and the tower and both aisles from the 14th century, the south aisle being added later than the north as the town grew. The chancel was renovated in the 19th century and has an oak screen and reredos of that time, though the sedilia with their rib vaulting and the piscina with its shelf are clearly medieval. The screen frames the 14th century font at the west end, resting on a still older base and decorated with coloured shields.

Nearby is a massive iron-bound parish chest with three padlocks. One of the clerestory windows is square-headed and rather odd-looking. The grooves in the columns are caused by sharpening arrow tips, and the squint in the south aisle chapel does not line up with the altar in the restored chancel. The Dixie tombs and memorials are in the north aisle and the marble nomument shows a sister mourning her beloved brother. A hatchment to another Dixie, Sir Willoughby Wolstan, which originally hung on the door of his house for a year after his death, is now suspended on the north wall opposite the main doorway. Interesting photographs of the church's interior, showing a singing gallery and tall box pews, are on view near the entrance.

(2) Sutton Cheney, at the foot of Ambion Hill, has moved away from its 13th century church of St James with its brick tower. The long, low nave must be little changed from the historic morning of 22nd August 1485, when the last of the Plantagenets heard his last mass there before going to his death on Bosworth Field. He, and those who fell with him are commemorated by a wall plaque put up by the Society of Richard III and flanked by the emblems of the White Boar and the White Rose of York. The same society has also presented a number of finely decorated kneelers and holds an annual memorial service every August as near as possible to the date of the battle.

The alabaster tomb of Sir William Roberts, owner of the Elizabethan manor opposite and founder of the row of almshouses, with the open dovecote at the end, is surmounted by the figures of his two wives in pious attitudes.

(3) The Battle Centre has an exhibition of the fearsome arms and flags of the period with models of the battle itself. It provides slide and film shows and outside is laid out a battle trail of nearly four miles with information boards, all of which makes for an interesting and evocative outing. There is a small cafe and bookstall to browse in.

Bosworth was the last great battle in the traditional medieval style. It took place on 22nd August 1485 and after an hour of fierce hand-to-hand fighting, Richard III had lost his life and his throne, and the Plantagenet line which began with Henry II came to an end.

The character of Richard, who is the central figure in the drama, is unfortunately much obscured by Tudor propaganda and the creation of Shakespeare. There is evidence that he was a capable administrator, a shrewd, skilful military commander and beyond any doubt, a very brave man. He was no more ruthless than any of his predecessors and it is now widely accepted that he in no way resembled the malevolent cripple portrayed by Shakespeare. He had an unbroken succession of military victories behind him and at Bosworth his personal courage contrasted markedly with the indecision and pusillanimity of his subordinates. He was badly served, save by a faithful few, but perhaps his earlier cruelties, misdeeds and mistakes made his own end , and that of his age, inevitable.

WALK 2

BRADGATE PARK – SWITHLAND WOOD – CROPSTON RESERVOIR

Distance 5 miles. O.S. Map No. 129 (Nottingham and Loughborough) 1:50,000. Start point Hallgates car park on B5330. Grid reference 545114

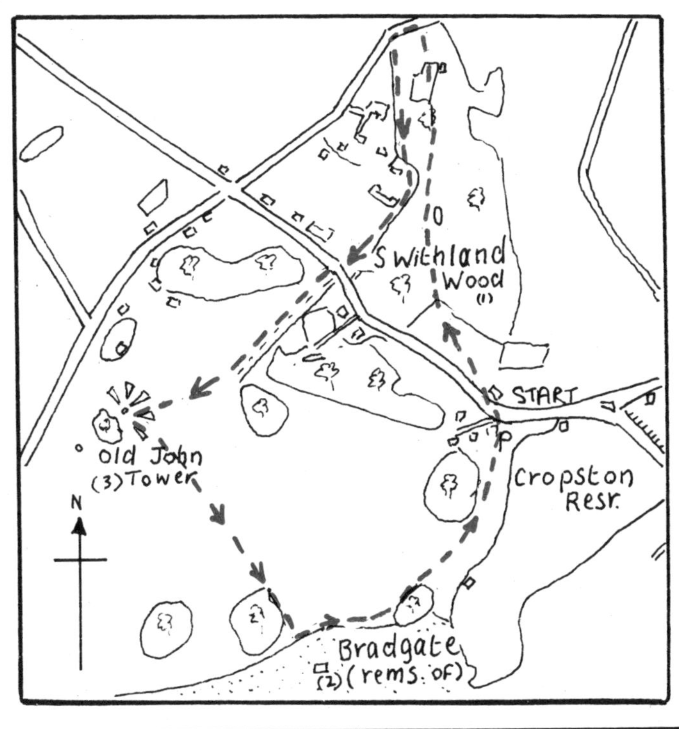

This is a walk first along the firm level tracks in the cool shade of Swithland Wood (1), then over the springy heathland of Bradgate Park (2), rising to 600 feet at Old John Tower (3) and finally descending to the reservoir at the Deer Barn. Cropston has a good choice of inns.

Starting from the car park, go left along the road past the farm, and over a stile on the right signposted Swithland, then diagonally left over the field to a foot-bridge of wooden beams in the corner. Cross into the wood and go uphill over a junction of tracks amid the bracken and beneath tall oaks and birch. At a broad stone track with yellow markers go left and uphill to the slate quarry and mounds. The path continues right past a plaque set up by the Leicester Rotary Club, and downhill curving among hazel and honeysuckle to an open glade. At an iron enclosure turn left past a slate barn, fork right and go up gently to another glade with beeches and a tall ash at the top. This is the wood edge with a view forwards. Follow the path left past another water-filled quarry to the road, turn left along it and come soon to a car park entry in the slate wall. Enter it and find the broad track going out from it into the wood again. Take it and gradually descend to another crossing track, where the way goes right and continues until it reaches a litter bin and bye-law notice board.

The first deep quarry is now off to the left, but the way goes right under birches and beeches to a gate by a wall. Turn left alongside a caravan site and go up by a chalet called 'Green View', then downhill for a short distance, left into the wood at a stile and immediately right. Old John Tower is in sight on the hill-top ahead. Descend to a foot-bridge and a hole in the wall to the road. Do not go left into the car park, but cross the road to a signpost for 'Old John'. The clear track now ascends alongside an arable field with reservoir buildings on the left to a tall kissing gate, and goes on among the bracken, rising up to the tower on its rocky outcrop with a toposcope nearby.

Face the way you have come, and the path down goes half right through a stand of oaks between three woods. The springy turf is starred with tiny four-petalled yellow tormentils. Go through a gateway in a wall and to the Deer Barn. . The ruins of Bradgate House are on the left, the reservoir ahead, and a metalled track also on the left leads straight back to Hallgates car park and the Reservoir Inn.

(1) Swithland Wood presents a landscape of ancient pollarded oaks and strange, often grotesque rocky outcrops, evidence of volcanic activity almost 600 million years ago. It is also a region where little change has occurred; it has never been cultivated, and the pollarded oaks are survivors of the old medieval forests. According to local legend, they were pollarded by a parker following the tragic death of Lady Jane Grey. Swithland Wood was presented to the city and county in 1931 by the Rotary Club of Leicester. Many of its oaks, as elsewhere in Charnwood Forest, were felled for use in making iron during the 18th century. Its slate quarries were opened in the 13th century, being widely used for roofs and tombstones until the 19th century when cheaper, mass-produced Welsh slates became the vogue. They are quiet, brooding places today, their sheer rocky flanks rising from the deep pools of steely grey water and surrounded by mounds which make them dangerous to approach.

(2) Bradgate Park, an area of almost 900 acres, has been a deer park since the 13th century, and red and fallow deer still browse near the ruins of Bradgate House, or around the edge of the reservoir where their

winter fodder is stored in the Old Deer Barn. Bradgate House was built as a hunting lodge by Thomas Grey, the first Marquis of Dorset, in about 1500. It showed the effect of the peaceful years following the protracted Wars of the Roses. It was one of the earliest manor houses to be built of bricks which were made on the site, and was without fortifications. The second Marquis, another Thomas Grey, was a close friend of the young Henry VIII and his son Henry married Lady Frances Brandon, the daughter of the Duke of Suffolk and granddaughter of Henry VII. Their first child, the Lady Jane, was born at Bradgate in October 1537 and grew up there, educated by Roger Ascham and John Aylmer. She was accomplished in Greek and Latin and fluent in French and Italian. From Bradgate she corresponded with Erasmus during his brief stay at Cambridge.

Unfortunately her direct descent from the founder of the Tudor dynasty made her an obvious pawn in the political ambitions of her scheming relatives. At sixteen she was married to Lord Guildford Dudley the son of the Regent and Lord Protector, the Duke of Northumberland.

When it was certain that the young King Edward VI could not long survive, Northumberland induced him to bequeath the throne to Lady Jane rather than to his half-sister, Mary Tudor. In 1553 on the death of the King, Lady Jane was proclaimed Queen by her father-in-law, but when the City of London and the country gentry, fearing a return to the unsettled days of civil war, declared for Mary, Lady Jane was arrested with her husband and both were later executed after the failure of Wyatt's rebellion. She died at the age of sixteen after a reign of only a few days, an innocent victim of the ambition and cruelty of others. The house was gutted by fire in 1694, and was allowed to fall into final ruin in the 18th century, although the Greys as Earls of Suffolk and later Earls of Stamford continued to hunt the deer park right down to the beginning of the present century.

(3) Old John Tower is a neo-Gothic folly erected in 1786 by the fifth Earl of Stamford in memory of a miller whose mill once stood on the site. According to local legend the Earl's eldest son was celebrating his coming of age with a bonfire built around a flagpole on the hill-top. The fire burned through the flagpole which fell on the unfortunate miller.

The tower was clearly built as a hunting lodge. A plaque commemorates Charles Bennion, the benefactor who bought Bradgate Park in 1928, and presented it to the City and County of Leicester for public recreation, on condition that it should be preserved with its wildlife unchanged. From the top of the hill, there are superb views over Charnwood Forest and the city of Leicester.

WALK 3

ASHBY ST. LEDGERS – BRAUNSTON – BARBY

Distances A.m. 3½ miles; p.m. approximately 4 miles. O.S. Map nos. 140 (Leicester and Coventry) and 152 (Northampton and Milton Keynes). Start point near Barby church. Grid reference 543703 on Sheet no. 140.

Alternative short route: Barby – Braunston – Barby. 5 miles.

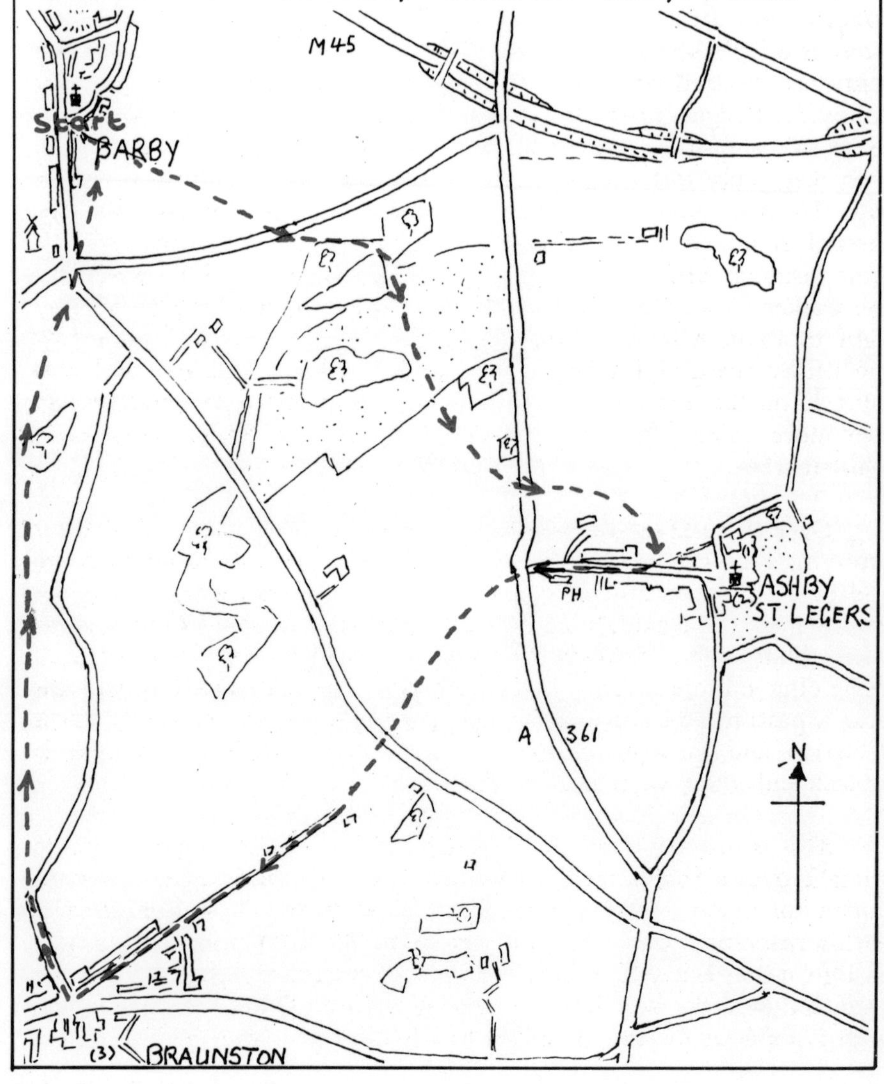

Walking in this part of Northamptonshire offers its own special rewards in the form of pleasantly undulating countryside bringing a succession of differing views, richly wooded parkland, extensive ridge and furrow betraying the whereabouts of long-forgotten settlements, and, in high summer, a profuse variety of wild flowers in the hedgerows. The roads are lined with noble ashes and though the scene is mainly rural, we are never far from the evidence of an industrial present and past in the shape of tall radio masts and winding canals.

Cars can be parked in Kilsby Road near Barby church, and opposite the Barn Shop and the junction of this road with the village street is a little seat on the left, convenient for walkers to change their footwear. Proceed left for about 100 yards to an indicated footpath for Ashby St. Ledgers near a bungalow. The path swings right by a wooden fence to a step-stile with a concrete step, the custom hereabouts, then goes diagonally left across two pastures and similar stiles to a white gate. Through this and over a stile on the left, it goes diagonally right through an arable field, over another stile, across another pasture on the same heading, with the Hill Morton radio masts on the left, and brings the walker to a stile in the right-hand corner. From here go sharper right to a stile half way along the hedge, then half left to a corner by the Kilsby road, and a finger post. A few yards to the left, under an ash tree on the right, is another stile into a field.. Look left and pick up two more stiles, where the route is indicated by black arrows on a white marker.

Over these stiles the way ahead skirts a wood, a safe refuge for scurrying rabbits. Aim for the distant corner of this stand of sycamore and pine, where another wood protrudes to the left. Here, where the woods meet, is a gate, a black and white waymarker, and an angling lake. Sharp right through the gate and ahead in the shade, or mud depending on the season, is another gate. The way lies through this into a pasture and straight on, keeping the wood on the right, across a stream and through another gate, metal this time. Again there is a black and white waymarker.

This is lush parkland, and keeping the wood on the right, continue straight over a rough track. Here half left is a stand of limes, unpollarded for many a year. Go past these down to a gate in a tall hedge, with a reassuring black and white arrow on a tree. Pass through the gate and go uphill across the field with a barn on the right to yet another gate, and here the way lies half way left across a field of waving barley, with a pond on the left. It might be better if the corn is high to follow the tractor tracks through it to the other side and them proceed left down the edge to a double fence and foot-bridge over a stream. After this go half left again and uphill towards the road, where the village of Ashby St. Ledgers soon comes into sight.

Once on the road, reached by an iron gate, a footpath sign points left to the village across a meadow. Follow the direction indicated, slightly left to the hedge opposite where there is an unwired portion of the fencing. Cross, and follow the route slowly swinging right by an ash at the field corner to a green metal gate. On the left is another gate, and the ways leads through it and right, following the wire to a concrete step-stile.. An overgrown path leads through scrub to the road in the village close by a telephone box and the main entrance to the old manor house (1) and church (2).

Turn right and walk up the village street to the Olde Coach Inn where good refreshment is obtainable. The earnest walker can press on to Braunston (3), for both villages are interesting and have good inns. The route goes up the village street to the cross-roads and straight over, alongside a chestnut grove. Ridge and furrow is extensive hereabouts. Walk alongside three arable fields, keeping the hedge on the left until, at the top a view of Braunston and its spire opens out. At the road, turn right and, after 20 yards or so, at a tin shack, go left through a gate and down through more striking examples of ancient cultivation. This may well have been one of the open fields of the abandoned villages so common in this area. Keep going down the well-trodden track towards Braunston, and enter it through a council estate. Pass the Wheatsheaf and the Post Office to the Old Plough Inn on the right, a suitable alternative eating house. Through its car park at the rear and across the road is a signposted path to Barby. Go down past Ash Way and Countryside, a modern estate, and find a path and stile ahead into a field. Straight in front is a line of willows, with a precarious foot-bridge in the middle. Look back here, as there is a good view of Braunston's spire and old mill tower.

Black and white markers now signal the route, up the hedge on the right, towards some dead elms and a metal gate. The plateau here is at 125 metres. Through the gate keep the hedge on the left, to another gate. Keep going straight ahead towards Braunston Fields Farm, with a long red-brick barn on the left. Across a long ridge and furrow pasture bear slightly left to a gate, with the faithful black and white markers, near the house. Go half left to a stream and the field corner. This stream is the county boundary. Cross a foot-bridge and stile into the next pasture and follow the hedge and ditch on the left. Tiltups Holt Farm is away on a ridge to the right. Cross a steepish pasture to a group of dead elms, again with markers, keeping some oaks and ashes on the left. Go diagonally right and up a sloping meadow to a stile in the hedge and cross the small arable obliquely to the left. Keep half left over the next field, climbing to a stile near the left-hand corner. There is a last view of Braunston church before the next short pasture leads to the road. Go right, past the cricket field, and left at the cross-roads past the water tower and mill, to re-enter the village of Barby.

Alternatively, from Braunston, take the Barby road right near the Wheatsheaf, and walk along it past Fir Tree Farm. The ridge and furrow soon begins to appear and behind are the smoking stacks of Harbury Cement Works and the glistening, motionless canal. Suddenly, on the right where the road bends is the whole lay-out of the abandoned medieval village of Falcliff, its heaving mounds and grassy roads mute evidence of depopulation due to sheep running. Together with the deserted site of Wolfhamcote it does much to explain the preponderance of ancient tillage here and conjures up pictures of our rustic forbears going about their daily tasks in these fields.

The road goes on over Cleve's Hill to a junction, and then left past Barby nurseries to the water tower. This route might form a good option to the main walk, starting from Barby and taking the field path in the reverse direction to Braunston, with the spire to point the way ahead, and returning by this road after refreshment.

(1) The manor and church are at the end of the village street. Most of the cottages are 20th century which makes them younger than some of the trees in the park. The manor was for two centuries in the possession of the ill-fated Catesby family whose occasional forays into history brought upon them retribution of the severest kind. Their lives were the very stuff of tragedy. In the 15th century, William Catesby, the notorious "Cat" of the popular doggerel: "The Cat, the Rat, and Lovell the Dog, ruled all England under the Hog", was the favoured minister of Richard III whose emblem was a white boar. William shared his master's dismal end on Bosworth Field in 1485.

In the 17th century, Robert Catesby, forced to sell his Oxfordshire estates to pay the constant heavy fines imposed on him for recusancy, was eventually compelled to live with his mother at the manor of Ashby St. Ledgers. Warwickshire and Northamptonshire were, it seems, fertile breeding grounds for Catholic rebellion, and the story goes that the infamous Gunpowder Plot was hatched by Robert Catesby, Robert Wintour and others in the Elizabethan gatehouse of the manor of Ashby. Indeed the same gatehouse saw Robert Catesby and five desperate companions gallop beneath it after an exhausting 80 mile ride from London on the 5th November 1605, bringing the news of the complete failure of the attempt to destroy the King and his government. When all the conspirators had been weeded out and executed, there were, it is said, no more than two Catholic land-owning families left in the whole of Northamptonshire.

Sombre as its history may be, the Jacobean mansion with its stone and timber-framed Tudor gatehouse is now a peaceful backwater, standing in a splendid, well-tended park. It has had many owners since the Catesbys and undergone many changes. Sir Edwin Lutyens designed the courtyard buildings in 1909, in a style that does not clash with the original, and a black and white half-timbered house transported from Ipswich by the second Viscount Wimborne completes the ensemble which, in spite of some contrasts, does form a harmonious whole. The second Lord Wimbourne held office under Churchill in the war, and his father was Lord Lieutenant of Ireland in the troubles of 1916-1918. A previous interesting owner was Josiah Guest whose wealth came from the iron foundries of South Wales and who was one of the creators of the well-known and still flourishing firm of G.K.N.

(2) The church is fascinating in that it is adorned with many of the features that have embellished the English parish church over the centuries. It was re-fashioned by John Catesby in the 15th century and his original doorway is still in position, crowned with a fine ogee arch. The guide book says that the dedication is in honour of St. Leodegarius, an obscure Burgundian bishop – hence the second half of the village's name. The first half is a popular place name in the district, spelled 'Asbi' or 'Asebi' in Domesday, probably relating to the splendid ash trees that are so numerous hereabouts. When John Catesby built his new nave he placed in it the ancient black 12th century pews, together with the marvellous rood screen which rises up into the most delicate fan tracery skilfully executed in hard oak.

At its base are two Jacobean enclosed pews, which conceal the original colouring of the bottom panels of the screen, and all the walls show traces of early painting which, together with the stained glass, must have made the church's interior the wonder of the county. Over all towers the three-decker Jacobean pulpit, complete with clerk's seat in the front. Numerous memorial tablets adorn the chancel walls, but the chief glory of the place is the brasses of the Catesby family. Behind the communion rails, and not normally visible, lie the effigies of the previously mentioned William, the "ill-starred favourite of a monstrous King", if we are to believe Shakespeare, and his wife. There they are, faithfully represented in brass which gives complete details of the heraldic costume of the period. Most interesting however, and even thrilling, are the clear delineations of the features and hair, as sensitive and life-life as in the famous portrait of his master.

In the south aisle, beneath a ring in the floor, is a smaller brass of a kneeling knight, probably William's son, and alongside him full-length, likenesses of Thomas Stokes and his wife Elena. Outside, the churchyard has been levelled, but in the north wall is a blocked-up doorway, presumably once the Lord's entrance, as there is a corresponding door in the estate wall over which a glimpse of the house and park can be enjoyed. On the south side is an obelisk, and two tombs of the Viscounts Wimbourne by Lutyens, who also designed the row of thatched cottages opposite the Olde Coach and Horses.

(3) Braunston's inns, the Wheatsheaf and the Old Plough, bear witness to its agricultural past, for it was originally a farming community, with grazing for sheep and cattle. Sheep grazing on a large scale must have brought about the depopulation of the outlying hamlets, though together with cattle raising, it resulted in the production of wool and hides which lifted the standard of living above subsistence level. Its history was to undergo great changes with the development of transport, however, for it is in a key communications position both for roads and canals. The turnpike from London to Dunchurch had a toll-gate there and introduced a measure of new life and vigour into the community, but it is as a canal centre that the place is best known. In 1805 the Grand Union opened and the minor Midlands canals, like the Oxford–Coventry, unloaded their goods there on to large boats for onward conveyance on this great inland waterway.

For the space of 20 or 30 years, there was great prosperity and a population increase of considerable proportions. All the trades associated with canal traffic – masons, bricklayers, blacksmiths, wharf workers, saddlers and general labourers were all needed here, and many new stone houses were built to accommodate the newcomers. Nor was their spiritual welfare neglected, for largely through the fund-raising activities of the remarkable Rev. A. B. Clough, the church was enlarged and restored in 1849. This gentleman was also responsible during his long ministry for improvements in sanitation and education and was evidently one of the leading figures in the bustling community. The great spire, 150 feet high and an ever-present landmark, is a fitting memorial to his energy and achievement. At the height of the short-lived canal era, Braunston must have been a busy and prosperous place, but now it has assumed the mantle of a commuter village, though there is still some local light industry. The canal traffic has dwindled to a trickle – considerable at times – of holiday-makers seeking relaxation in long-boat cruising. A walk down the main street reveals the development of the village in the many different styles and materials of its buildings.

WALK 4

FAWSLEY PARK – BADBY – NEWNHAM – EVERDON – FAWSLEY PARK

Distance a.m. 3 miles, p.m. approximately 4 miles.
O.S. Map no. 152 (Northampton and Milton Keynes) 1:50,000.
Start point and car parking in Fawsley Park, grid reference 565569.

Scale
2cm
to
1km

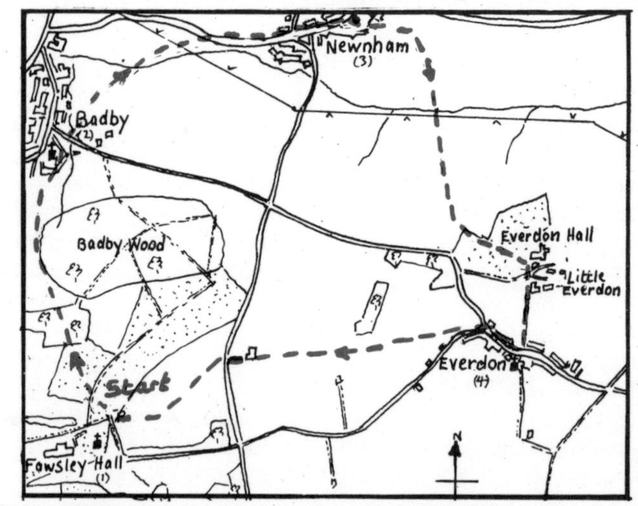

This is a pleasant, undulating walk through grassy parkland, a shady wood, and three pretty Northamptonshire villages. A little road walking, including a short, but not severe climb, gives excellent afternoon views. The rural landscape is dominated by fine tall trees and coloured, in summer, with extensive grain fields.

Enter the Park and pass on the right the Hall, former home of the Knightley family (1). The road descends, goes left by a lake with Fawsley church on the right, and just round the corner are some tall beeches forming a convenient parking and starting point. A circular white marker slightly to the left ahead at a stile indicates the path which skirts a wire fence with an oak on the right to another stile in front. It winds on through a cornfield to a tall stile leading into parkland. There is a fine view behind the house and its two stately cedars. A double line of oaks crosses the way which rises up to a stand of beeches. Another white marker with a blue base on an oak indicates not only the route, but also an elaborate badger sett where the industrious creatures have thrown up huge quantities of the brown earth.

At a dead elm, another marker beckons onwards to a wire fence at the park's edge. Over the stile in the fence the way goes diagonally left across the cornfield to a spinney in the right-hand corner. Enter it and look for a hunting gate immediately on the right. Follow the path down through shady glades past another marker on a sycamore. The bracken and willow herb thrive on the cool moistness. Just past a huge sweet chestnut is another extensive badger sett and a small stream on the right. The path soon comes to the wood edge, giving a preview of Badby church(2).

A fallen elder lies across the way which emerges from the wood at a step-stile. Over the clumps of blackberries to the left, the church tower rises, and the way crosses a delightful meadow to another stile. On entering the second meadow with Badby Wood on the right, look for a tall sycamore on the left, overshadowing the short rising path to Badby village, where it emerges at a sign-post indicating the Knightley Way in the reverse direction.

Turn right to the sloping village green with its chestnut tree and post box. Take the road – Brookside Lane – which goes down right, past a house with a plaque TC 1722. The Youth Hostel is on the left, and the lane dips steeply and veers left, embracing the village. Soon it goes left again and comes to a red-brick chapel. Just before this at a small silver birch on the right, take the path along the left-hand edge of a cornfield with a stream and some houses on the left. After a couple of hundred yards, it reaches a foot-bridge on the left and goes sharply off at right-angles through the middle of the corn to another foot-bridge and stream near a willow and ash. It then continues alongside the infant river Nene, with a farm and road on the left, until it reaches another foot-bridge consisting of a narrow railway sleeper, still hugs the Nene across the next field, and finally passes beneath some power lines to reach the road. Turn right here and walk into the village of Newnham (3) entering it by a green overhung with sycamores.

The excellent Romer Arms on the right offers food every day except Monday, when the village shop next door is very useful. After refreshment, go right, through the village and past the school, towards the church on a hill. Just before reaching it, take the lane on the right – Manor Lane – which gradually descends, leaves the houses and becomes a concrete track going past the 'Nuttery', and veers right to a sewage works. Go left where it bends right, and continue ahead through two pastures to a large oak with a gate in the corner on the right. Pass through this and downhill with the hedge and a barn on the left to a foot-bridge at a tall pylon. Cross, and keep ahead through the fields and two gates, with the hedge and a small stream on the right, to a depression in the ground – possibly the stream source. The route now becomes indistinct, but go diagonally left over the ridge and furrow to a corner stile, then skirt the arable field by the right edge, going left at the top to come out on to the parkland at Little Everdon. The Hall is on the left, and a gate on the right admits to the park. Cross it, going gradually left, and find a white gate on the far side near which stands the public footpath sign for Newnham. This is the hamlet of Little Everdon, a charming cluster of brown stone cottages, with one large house bearing the initials F.W.T 1690. Turn right up the lane to

Everdon itself (4). Leave the pub and church on the left and walk up the main street to a long row of cottages on the right, opposite the old red-brick smithy, where a lane goes off to the left and climbs steeply.

There is now a choice of ways – either the gated lane which rises up to give superb views of the village and beyond, or a marked field path high in the hedge on the right to Fawsley. The former arrives after two kilometres at a crossroads, where the right turn soon brings the walker to the point where the field path joins the road. The latter follows the hedge boundary on the left up a steep pasture and across three grain fields, an exhilarating climb with even better views. After the third grain field, which has a stile in the left corner, follow the white arrows across a rough pasture down to a tall ash, then cross the next meadow to the road, keeping the farm on the right. Now take the signposted path for Fawsley across the road – it rises up through sheep pastures to Temple Hill, and then descends to the left to a gate. Go through a second gate on the right and return to the parking place.

(1) The Knightleys were in possession of Fawsley for 500 years, but the last baronet died in 1938, since when the continued existence of the house built by Sir Edmund in the 16th century has often been imperilled. It still stands intact, its central hall and fine oriel window flanked by rather nondescript wings in the colourful Northamptonshire stone. The Knightleys came from Staffordshire in the 15th century and founded their wealth, which was never ostentatious, on sheep. They grazed their flocks in neighbouring Charwelton parish and certainly emparked the village of Fawsley, leaving the 13th century church of St. Mary standing in splendid isolation facing their great house. What happened to the displaced villagers is another story, but the Knightleys rapidly became accepted as county nobility though they were never nationally famous, save when Sir Richard became involved in the publication of anti-Popish tracts directed at people in high places, suspected by him of Popery in the 1580s. Though heavily fined, he recovered favour enough to be chosen as one of those who witnessed the execution of Mary, Queen of Scots. Another Sir Richard was a close friend of Pym, Hampden and leading Parliamentarians. Overweening ambition was not one of their vices, and if they made a modest fortune out of miseries inflicted on the peasantry by sheep running and emparking, they were doing no more than many other nouveau-riche families, like the Spencers and must be judged by the standards of their times.

The little church is now a shrine to their memory, containing a fine brass in the floor beneath which Sir Edmund lies, and an equally impressive tomb of one of the many Sir Richards, knighted by Henry VIII, with his eight sons and four daughters in mourning attitudes beneath his effigy.

(2) Badby, which claims to be one of the prettiest villages in the county, as do many of its neighbours, is spacious and grouped round a green. Opposite the church is a fine house in local stone with mullioned windows, rather spoiled though by its ugly roofing. The church is light and airy, mainly Early English with a beautiful decorated clerestory of ten windows, The last pillar on the north side has an in-built piscina with an encircling band of ball flower ornamentation above. In the restored chancel are sedilia and another piscina with a petalled drain. The fine oak pulpit has a hinged door and a candle-holder. Light streaming through the clerestory illuminates the coloured pillars and adds to the sense of space and airiness. The church was part of the holdings of Evesham Abbey, later belonged to Christ Church, Oxford, and later still was endowed with Knightley charities.

(3) Newnham has space and fine houses in plenty, many with steep-pitched roofs originally designed to allow rain water to run off the thatch without penetrating it. Its inn was burned down in the thirties and rebuilt by the local squire whose name it bears. A charming American couple keep it, and in its well-tended garden is the old village bakehouse.

The church has a tall open spire with arches of the 15th century. Its exterior is not as fine as that of Badby, but high up in the east wall is an old sanctus bell turret. The original roof of thatch was replaced when the 15th century clerestory was added. Inside are high box pews, and a link with the Catesbys of Ashby St. Ledgers – a 15th century memorial brass to Letitia, second wife of Robert Catesby who died in 1467. From early times the Catesbys, Knightleys and Thorntons have been the leading families in the district.

(4) 'Everdon' in old English meant 'Boar's Hill' and the noble church, which dwarfs those of neighbouring parishes, was entirely rebuilt in the decorated style in the early 14th century – striking evidence of the prosperity of the area, doubtless founded on wool, but also on its close association with the rich Norman abbey of Bernay.

The village has a long street lined with high banks and shaded by tall limes. Still remote, it must have been even more so when the uncle of the poet Thomas Grey was vicar here for sixteen years until his death in 1742. His memorial stone is set in the sanctuary floor. It was to the care of this William Antrobus that Grey was entrusted by his mother, who feared for his survival and sought to protect him from his brutal father. Here in his formative years he must often have heard the lowing herds, seen the ploughman wending his weary way home, and contemplated the narrow cells of the hamlet's forefathers in the churchyard as he gathered those thoughts and sentiments that were later to inspire his haunting, beautiful and nostalgic elegy.

WALK 5

SHUCKBURGH PARK

Distance 5 miles.
O.S. Map No. 151 (Stratford-upon-Avon), 1:50,000
Start point and car park Lower Shuckburgh church. Grid ref. 489627.

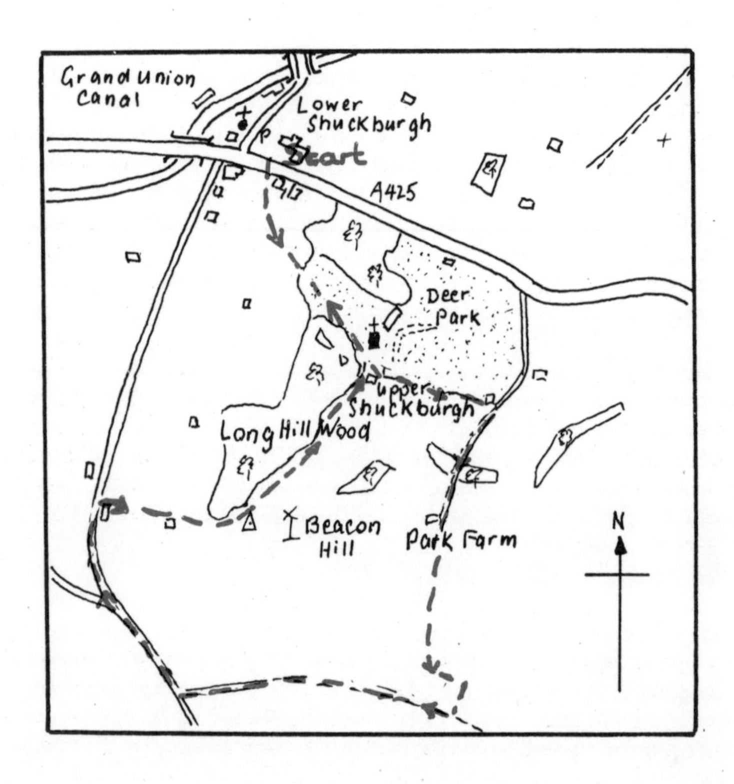

This charming little walk on the Warwickshire/Northamptonshire border can be completed well in time for lunch at the inn on the main road in Napton, or at the Countryman, Staverton. Alternatively, it can be done as an afternoon ramble. The scenery provides a change from the flat Warwickshire arable and consists mainly of hilly pasture in the park which is nicely wooded and landscaped, affording good views and supporting a good variety of wild life. Lower Shuckburgh is at 300 feet,

Beacon Hill at 678 – modest, but respectable for these parts. The Hall is the home of Sir Charles Shuckburgh and together with its church is of course, private property, but the rights of way are clearly marked, leaving no excuse for deviation from the route.

Roadside parking for a car or two is available in the lane near the "sugar plum" Victorian church of Lower Shuckburgh, just off the A425. The interior of this building boasts a fine display of coloured brick. Across the main road and to the left of a stone cottage is a stile with a yellow marker pointing uphill towards two white gates near a farm. Through the gates the way winds gently up amid the ridge and furrow of the ancient settlement, emparked long ago and enclosed within the estate, towards a stark dead elm slightly to the left. There is a kissing gate, also with an arrow, and from this vantage point a view extends to the rear over the little hamlet and the flatlands beyond.

Continue past a grassy slope on the left riddled with rabbit warrens and leading up to a wood of tall oaks. Ahead, where fine beeches crown the summit, is a gate, with a notice warning to keep dogs under control, and on the right, occupied by water fowl, is a large man-made pool and island. To the left is a wooded knoll surrounded by a beech hedge which encloses the little church, peculiar in that it belongs to no diocese but is entirely private. Private too is the house nearby. The way goes over the brow and dips towards a farm encircled by a herd of gentle Jerseys, each sporting her own yellow collar. Different views now open up to the front as the way goes down a gravel track alongside a high red-brick wall with the farm buildings on the right. In the distance a herd of grey deer can sometimes be seen, dotting the park like fallen leaves.

At the extremity of the deer park near a lodge on the left turn sharp right along a bridle path. There is a final view to the rear of the church and Hall before the metalled track bounded by iron railings crosses a culvert and passes a grove of firs and oaks, to arrive at Park Farm with more ridge and furrow on the left. Usually, Charolais cattle are peacefully grazing in the fields ahead where two dead elms again provide a direction market for a stile. Over this the way now follows a tall hedge, goes through a muddy gap, and swings left along the field boundary towards an iron gate and two ashes, then right along the side of the arable to a broken gate. A grassy track now goes to the right – forming not only the county boundary, but that of the European constituency as well. It soon becomes a stony road with power lines on its left, and is flanked by a line of ashes very reminiscent of other walks in Northamptonshire. Go through the gates and straight on for about half a mile to a road, and turn right to a T-junction. Napton sits prettily on its hill to the left, but the route lies along the road to Lower Shuckburgh – straight on for about twenty yards or so.

Just past Halls Barn Farm, the first house on the right, is a stile with its arrow pointing diagonally across the arable towards a low huddle of red barns. Follow the direction indicated over the sticky surface and through two gates ahead,then go upwards with the wood on the left. On this side is a fine stand of beeches and pines, and on the right further over is a trig. point and wind pump. This is Beacon Hill and it has good views in every direction. The going across the high pasture is excellent and the air exhilirating. The downward route passes through two gates, and, leaving some pheasant feeding pens on the left, bends slightly leftwards past a knoll until the church comes into sight again. It is now a simple matter to retrace steps down the slope gradually losing height until the main road and Victorian church are within sight.

The parish was enclosed very early on and from an inquisition of 1517 we learn that the Prioress of Wroxall, together with Thomas Catesby, and one Thomas Shuckburgh had shared in this process. The latter was alleged to have intended to lay the whole township to pasture, according to the Victoria County History, which declares that depopulation quickly followed, and has continued. The ridge and furrow is everywhere apparent. Upper Shuckburgh is now almost entirely taken up by the park and grounds of the estate. Celia Fiennes, passing through on her way to Daventry in 1697, found 'Nether Shuzar' a sad village, but was rescued from her tedium by Sir Charles who entertained her in the Hall, which she describes as being "very handsome, built of brick and stone".

Shuckburghs or de Shuckburghs, have been prominent in these parts since the beginning of the 12th century. They were tax collectors, coroners and Justices for Warwickshire in the 15th and 16th centuries. Sir Richard, who lived from 1606–56, was M.P. for the county. It is of him that the well-known story is told, that whilst out hunting on Beacon Hill he was observed by Charles I on his way to Edge Hill on 22nd October 1642. The King was moved to ask who this was thus taking his pleasure whilst great events of state were stirring, and commanded the huntsman to appear before him. So gracious was His Majesty in his reception of this errant subject that the latter was persuaded to return home at once, arm his retainers and fight for his King next day, to such good effect that he was knighted after the battle. Later he fortified his house and defended it against Parliament, only to be wounded and captured. A prisoner at Kenilworth, he lived long enough to see his master's bitter end, and his loyalty cost him dear. After the Restoration, his son John was created baronet by Charles II in 1660, and his estates have thereafter descended in continuous line. Generations of the family are commemorated in the little church near the house, surrounded by fine cedars. The church itself was largely reconstructed in the 1660s after being despoiled by Cromwell's men, and since then, like the family, it has continued its quiet course through history.

WALK 6

RADWAY – EDGE HILL – HORNTON – RATLEY – RADWAY

Distances a.m. 4½ miles, p.m. approximately 3 miles.
O.S. Map No. 151 (Stratford-upon-Avon) 1:50,000
Start point and car park – Radway church. Grid reference 368481

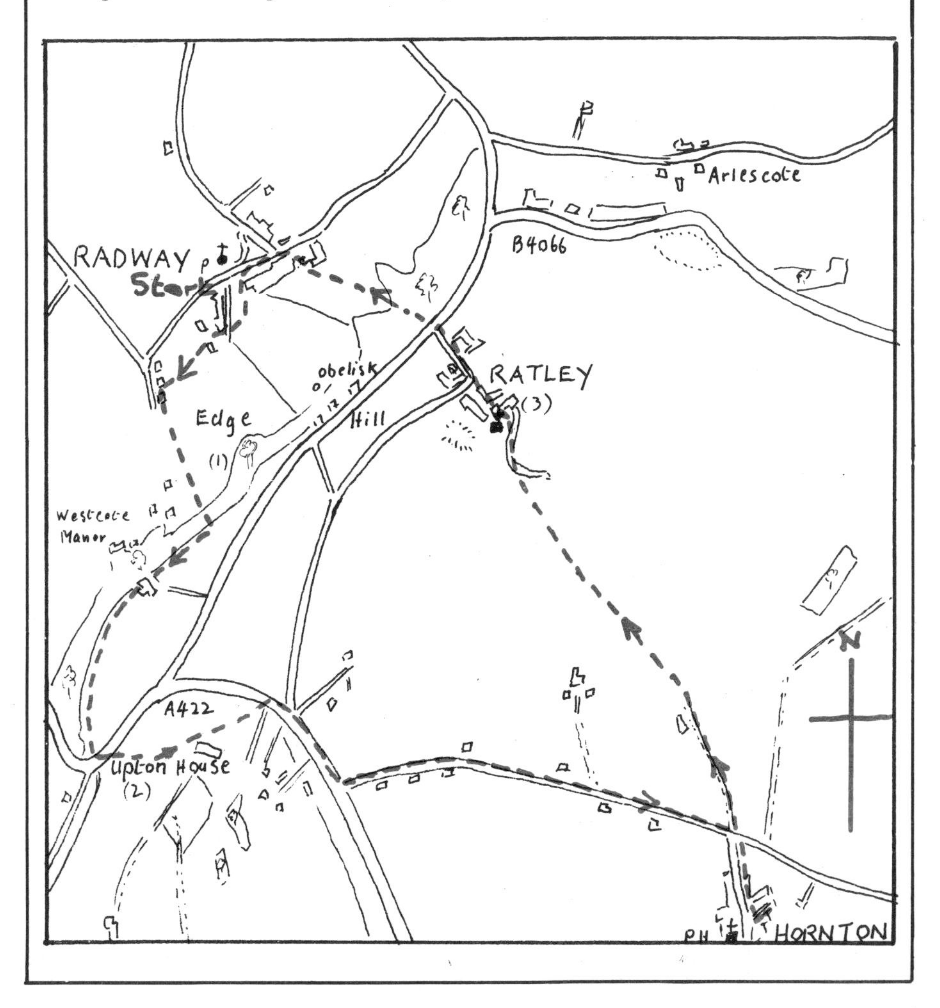

The real pleasures of this walk lie in the splendour of the views from the top of Edge Hill (1) and the enjoyment of climbing the escarpment in each direction, the charm of the brown ironstone cottages at Radway (2), the vista of the drive to Upton House (3) behind its graceful wrought-iron gateway and the friendly welcome at the Dun Cow in Hornton. The ancient church and inn at Ratley (4) form the main points of interest of the return route.

From Radway church, take the road leading to the green at the top of the village, where two houses with corrugated iron roofs come into view. Alongside the right-hand one runs a narrow path bordered by ancient gravestones. Here stood the first village church existing at the time of the battle in 1642, but the site is now sorely neglected. A stile leads to a meadow, and then to another with an old barn. On the left is ridge and furrow. Walk along the headland, keeping to the left of the barn, which, according to an excellent pamphlet, 'Edge Hill Nature Trail', published by Warnact, dates from around 1600. Come to a gate by a house ahead, and turn left up the lane which can be a quagmire of yellow clay in wet weather. This is King John's Lane, an ancient holloway with high hedges of great age, possibly the route down to the plain taken by the Royalist army. It leads, after a steep and muddy ascent, to the ridge top. After a pause for breath and to admire the splendid view, take the path to the right, at 480 feet, which follows the edge of the wood and skirts arable fields to the left. Here are clear signs of badger activity – scrapes, latrines and great setts in the loamy soil.

Continue along the crest to the lane leading to Westcote Manor Farm. Pass through the stone pillars and go right by a wall to the next significant feature – the A422 passing over Sunrising Hill, which commands a magnificent view over the Feldon. Turn left up the busy road for a short way until on the right you see a tree-lined track. Just after this a signposted route leads along a drystone wall to a gate where the way goes diagonally left across the pasture, keeping to the left of the farm buildings set in a fold of the ground. Now look for two lift-off gates on the left, facing each other. Through them is a meadow with a wire fence on the left. To the right are the hummocks of a deserted village and the drive to the Home Farm of Upton House.

Come to the road, turn right, and pass before the entrance drive of the house. Continue along the road to a junction and take the lane to the left for about a mile, and then turn right down to Hornton in its sheltered valley. It is a lovely Oxfordshire village with a green at the bottom of the hill. The Dun Cow is off to the right of the green and the landlord, a walker himself, told us over an excellent lunch that there were once five pubs here.

Retrace steps afterwards up the hill to the lane junction and go straight over and along the farm track, past barns and a water tower on stilts. The way rises and then drops to a gate. Cross the arable field ahead – very sticky in winter – to the little footbridge over the stream on the further boundary, and then go up the next meadow to a metal gate at the top where a track leads past the church and on to the village of Radley.

Turn right at a junction towards the village shop, where a flight of stone steps leads to a pasture with drystone walling and a stone boundary stile at the top ahead. Thence a farm track goes left to the road.

Turn right, past a group of modern stone houses and a football field, and continue to the road overlooking Edge Hill. Now descend the steps on the other side of the road and emerge from the trees to enjoy the panorama spread out ahead. Then coast down the slope and, keeping to the right, find a stile and path leading directly to the road in Radway village.

(1) This is country rich in history, and once rich in mineral wealth, as the iron and stone working on Edge Hill prove. The celebrated Hornton stone is still quarried and is much in demand for building purposes. The houses of Radway, Hornton and Ratley, constructed almost entirely from this material, which ranges in colour from yellow to dark ochre, blend harmoniously with the brown clay soil and the soft greens of the fields, and gracing the whole are the two fine country seats of Farnborough and Upton House, now both in the care of the National Trust.

On the side of the road from Kineton stands the small inscribed monument to the 500 men killed in the battle and buried nearby. Their grave is unapproachable, as is the site of the struggle, fierce but indecisive, that took place here that Sunday in 1642. The place is still given up to war and to preparations for war. The eye is easily carried to the slopes beyond, down which Rupert's cavalry – watched by the King from the summit, then bare of trees – thundered into the Roundhead foot, scattering them in confusion as far as Kineton, only to return too late to the main scene of action. Ghosts are still said to stalk these hills, and men still like to affect the uniforms, manners and arms of those days. Yet there was little romance in this incident, but only the beginnings of that divisive bitterness characteristic of Civil War.

(2) At Radway, one can be forgiven for thinking oneself in the 19th or even 18th century. The long row of thatched cottages can have changed little in appearance since the days of 'Lark Rise to Candleford', One can easily envisage the smock-clad labourers rising to tend their pigs at dawn before setting off for the day-long toil in the fields. The Grange, situated discreetly behind its trees, has had its moments in history. It was purchased in 1715 by Sanderson Miller from its previous owner Thomas Goodwin. Sanderson Miller the son inherited it in 1735. He was architect, landscape artist, 'improver', and well-known Warwickshire worthy. In his time many were the celebrated visitors to the house. The great Chatham planted trees in the grounds, and listened to Henry Fielding, whose family lived at nearby Newnham Paddox, reading from his novel 'Tom Jones' in the drawing room.

Sanderson Miller enjoyed the friendship of the great, and had more than a local reputation for innovations in agricultural matters. It was he who planted the tall beeches which now crown the escarpment, and he regularly rode over to Farnborough Hall to dine with its owner William Holbech. Together they planned improvements in the Hall and grounds, including the magnificent terrace with its Ionic temple, pavilion, obelisk and game parlour. He also built the octagonal tower on Edge Hill top as a point of vantage and place of entertainment for his friends. It is now incorporated in the inn. His descendants remained at Radway until the last of them died in 1910. He was the Rev. William Sanderson Miller, last of a long line of vicars, for the family combined the functions of both squire and parson throughout the 19th century and the Rev. George, great great grandson of the first Sanderson Miller, wrote a fascinating book full of family anecdotes and local lore entitled 'Rambles round the Edge Hills'.

It appears that Field Marshal Earl Haig also made his home in the village, for he is listed on a memorial in the lychgate of the church among those who returned safely from the Great War. The church itself was rebuilt in 1866, replacing an earlier structure of simple design, and contains the mutilated effigy in full military dress of the period, of Captain Henry Kingsmill who fell in the battle.

(3) The delicate tracery of the wrought-iron grille surmounted by the initial 'B', and the long gravel approach to the rear of Upton House create an excellent impression of good taste. It is the seat of the Lords Bearsted and is now a National Trust property housing a magnificent collection of porcelain and paintings. The building is in the local brown stone, with a long facade and lawns fronting a steep drop to a lake. The Victoria County History says that the place-name Upton gave its name to a family, the de Uptons, who owned the manor in the time of Henry VI. It then passed through the hands of the Verney family to one Wm. Danvers who sold it to Sir Rushout Cullen, M.P. for Cambridgeshire 1697–1710. His son was responsible for re-building the house in a manner suitable to his dignity, a task completed in 1695 as is evinced by the initials 'R. C. 1695' on the lead rainwater heads on the south side. It was finally acquired, after many vicissitudes, by the second Lord Bearsted in 1927. His father had, from humble beginnings, created the huge Shell company, whose activities came to include world-wide interests in transport and petroleum, and as the founder of this empire he was ennobled in 1921. His son became a philanthropist and collector, and Upton was made the home, not only of his family, but of his collection of works of art of all kinds, especially paintings and porcelain of Sevres and Chelsea. On his death in 1948, both house and

collection were bequeathed to the National Trust, and the present Lord Bearsted is still in residence.

(4) The church at Ratley, of St. Peter ad Vincula – St. Peter in chains – dates from about 1340, but there was probably an earlier place of worship on the site. It was restored in 1872,and is spacious and well-lit. Restoration is currently proceeding again, with the replacement of the stonework round the windows. It is a quiet, ancient place well worth visiting. Seventeen men of the name of England are recorded on a tablet in the church as having served in the Great War, and four of them, Shem, Ernest, Ralph and Edward, fell, and are commemorated on the memorial in the churchyard, together with Richard who was killed in the last war.

The Rose and Crown, a low-ceilinged stone house of great antiquity with an attractive sign, is a free house with a good assortment of ales. Inside, beneath the low oak beams, and against the background of the huge open fireplace, the landlord said he thought it dated from the 11th century and was built as a place of shelter for the workmen busy constructing the first church – an interesting theory, impossible to check on.

LOWER BRAILES – CHERINGTON – SUTTON-UNDER-BRAILES – LOWER BRAILES

Distances a.m. 3½ miles, p.m. approximately 2½ miles.
O.S. Map No. 151 (Stratford-upon-Avon), 1:50,000
Start point and car parking – St. George's Church, Lower Brailes.
Grid reference 316393.

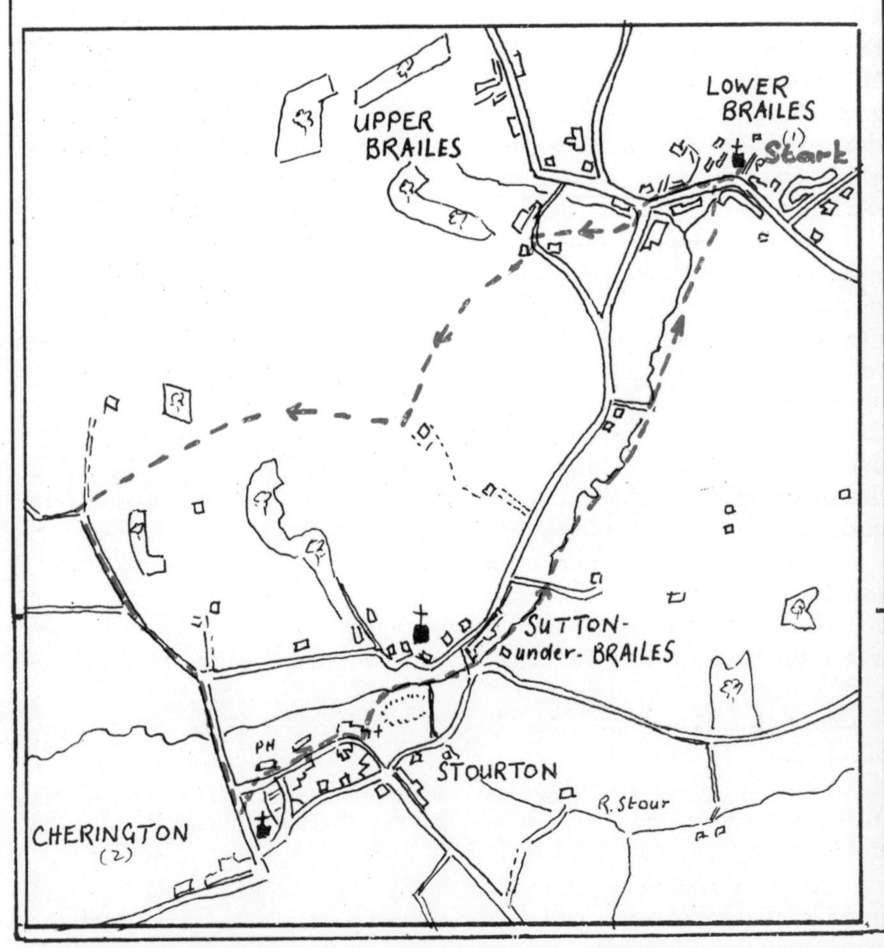

This ramble near the Warwickshire/Oxfordshire border comprises a delightful morning walk over the ridge of Brailes Hill which rises to 700 feet, giving extensive views over Upper and Lower Brailes (1), with good firm going on sheep pasture and ridge and furrow before a gradual descent through hazel scrub and along lanes to Cherington (2) for lunch. The afternoon route is flat and easy, following the meanderings of an infant tributary of the Stour with Mine Hill rising up on the right, and visiting the hamlet of Sutton-under-Brailes on the left. The going here can be muddy in winter, but otherwise no undue exertion is necessary.

From the church, go right and downhill past the George and Post Office, then up past the garage, a road junction, and the modern school. On the right are visible the earthworks on Castle Hill. Soon, just beyond a letter-box, go left up Henbrook Lane past the thatched houses. Grove End has a particularly steep-pitched roof. Pass in front of a long white house on the right where a broken sign-post indicates the way. The path goes to the left of a flight of concrete steps, becomes rapidly overshadowed and can be miry, but soon dries out higher up. This is the gentle ascent to the ridge of Brailes Hill and soon the views open out on the left over the village and beyond into Oxfordshire.

There are two iron gates to pass through before emerging on to the ridge and furrow with a pond below and on the left. Now go down through a gate gap and up to a group of farm buildings – keep to the right under the oaks, then bear hard right through another gate-gap and follow the left-hand edge of the arable field towards a low line of pollarded willows. In the valley on the left the bells of Sutton or Cherington will probably be ringing. Continue along the field edge under a group of tall poplars to a metal gate and go straight ahead through two more gates to a fence and stile in the right-hand corner under a tall hawthorn.

From here, go directly across two sheep pastures, each with gates, and descend through a facing hedge gap to another gate admitting to a belt of scrub hawthorn The ground drops through a pasture to a lane, where the way is left and straight on to a junction past a red-brick farm with a weather-cock, and a stone house with noisy dogs. Go straight on – Cherington ¾ – past Little Butts, then right to a bridge over the Stour, and left by a stone house to the inn. The church is ahead on a slight hill, and for those visiting it, the way to the cheerful Cherington Arms, which provides good ale and sandwiches, is back across the ridge and furrow at the rear of the church to the road.

After refreshment, go left down the road towards an imposing stone house with three gables and two tall chimneys, on the left of which is a path leading under a yew tree past the Methodist Chapel, built in 1809. Step over a stile and Sutton-under-Brailes is already in sight. Go down to the stream, Sutton Brook, but ignore at your peril the friendly ponies and donkeys. Feed them, or else be followed along the line of willows and over a bridge between gates. Go half right here to a gate and road, and left up the road under tall ashes to the outskirts of Sutton-under-Brailes. Turn right before the green at a house with staddle stones and walk down a sign-posted tarmac lane.

There is a step-stile on the left at the land's end and the way goes over it across the meadow to a double stile. Cross this and look for a flimsy foot-bridge on the right over the stream. This can be awkward, especially in flood, so negotiate with care, and go left along the stream bank past ashes and hawthorns to a stile and gate. Continue straight over the track and stile ahead. Now skirt the arable field under the huge willows with the flank of Mine Hill rising up on the right. There is a double fence stile, a ditch near two oaks, and suddenly, Brailes tower breaks magnificently into view. Go through two gates and stay on the same heading, skirting ploughlands until finally going left over the stream to a wall, where a path bends to the right and leads to the main road opposite the church.

(1) Brailes straddles the B4035 and is overlooked by the dominant features of Castle Hill with its earthworks to the north, the long ridge of Brailes Hill to the south-west and Mine Hill to the south-east. The large straggling parish, consisting of Upper and Lower Brailes, lies on the borders of Oxfordshire, from which it is separated by a long ridgeway known locally as Beggar's Lane. In the later Middle Ages it was clearly a town of fair size, wealth and importance, a market centre for the prosperous wool trade. In 1248, it had been granted a weekly market and a three day annual fair, "on the eve, day and morrow of St. George's day", and according to a local document, by the middle of the 15th century, "the parishe ys of greate compasse, and hath almost 2000 houselyng people". There is still some evidence of old roads and ancient house foundations around both Upper and Lower Brailes.

The earthworks at Castle Hill on the north side of Upper Brailes are considerably eroded, and, it has been claimed, are the remains of a castle built here by a 12th century Earl of Warwick who owned the manor. There is, however, no record in writing of such a fortification.

In addition to the Beauchamp family, who were granted it by Henry I, the manor has known as its owners the Fiennes, the Lords Clinton and Say, and a branch of the de Montforts, whose Lord, Peter, fell at the battle of Evesham in 1265. Later it came into the possession of the Spencers and the Marquis of Northampton. The secret of its importance is the same as that of most Cotswold townships – sheep. By the 14th century it was the third biggest market town in the County of Warwickshire, with water mills and a thriving trade in wool, in spite of severe setbacks caused by the Black Death and subsequent plagues. Its prosperity, as always with wool towns such as Winchcombe and

Chipping Campden, is mirrored in its magnificent and justly famous church of St. George, dating largely from the same period. Nowadays there are few signs of the village's past in the shape of vernacular buildings, but in Lower Brailes the George Inn is of pleasant stone with mullioned windows of the 16th century, whilst in Upper Brailes, which is mainly red brick, the Gate Inn is also a pleasing stone structure.

Non-conformity was strong, as often in busy centres of trade, and is evidenced by a Roman Catholic church, a Friends' Meeting House, open till 1850, and two Methodist chapels. The village was home to William Brailes, one of the few historical figures (Matthew Paris is another) known definitely as illuminators of 13th century manuscripts.

The 'Cathedral of the Feldon' which dominates the middle of the village is a most impressive building with a 13th century nave, a 14th century chancel and a most splendid 15th century perpendicular tower with battlements and pinnacles. Externally it is rugged and weather-beaten, with a long south aisle surmounted by a clerestory. The aisle has a flowing openwork parapet, with a series of carvings, some now almost unrecognisable in the crumbling sandstone, aligned along the string course. There are animal heads, ball flowers, female figures, and monsters all jostling each other below the stone water spouts. The great east window has tracery of the decorated style, whilst the south and west are perpendicular. The chief treasure of the interior is the 14th century font with each of its eight faces showing the window tracery designs popular in the period, and in the chancel, restored in ashlar in 1879, are two great free-standing candelabra, each having seven branching arms. These were intended to illuminate the altar in puritanical anti-Catholic days when no candles or even a cross were allowed on the sacred table. To the right of the altar the sedilia are set at different levels to correspond to the three stages of the medieval mass performed by the celebrant, the deacon and the subdeacon.

The north arcade and clerestory were extensively damaged, possibly in the Civil War, and rebuilt in the 17th century. Restoration again took place in 1879, but no amount of reconstruction can detract from the air of antiquity and authority surrounding the great building, especially when it is seen from a distance.

(2) Cherington is a quiet place of pleasant homes and a 13th century church, of St. John the Baptist, with some 15th century additions. The most interesting feature is the tomb-chest and effigy neatly fitted into their piercing, east of the nave arcade. The canopy and chest are of the decorated style of the early 14th century, the effigy that of a man in civilian costume. He is wearing an ankle-length gown with loose sleeves through which the raised arms reveal the tunic sleeves laced with points. Curiously there is no commemorative or armorial tablet on the tomb

and one can only assume that it is of a landowner of some means but of non-noble status, probably a franklin or steward.

The picturesque little hamlet of Sutton-under-Brailes with its attractive green was originally the property of the Saxon monastery of Deerhurst, and as a result, remained as a detached parish of Gloucestershire until 1840.

WALK 8

LONG COMPTON – LITTLE COMPTON – ROLLRIGHT STONES LONG COMPTON

Distance a.m. 3½ miles, p.m. approximately 4½ miles.
O.S. Map No. 151 (Stratford-upon-Avon), 1:50,000 Start point and car park in lane opposite Long Compton church. Grid reference 288329.

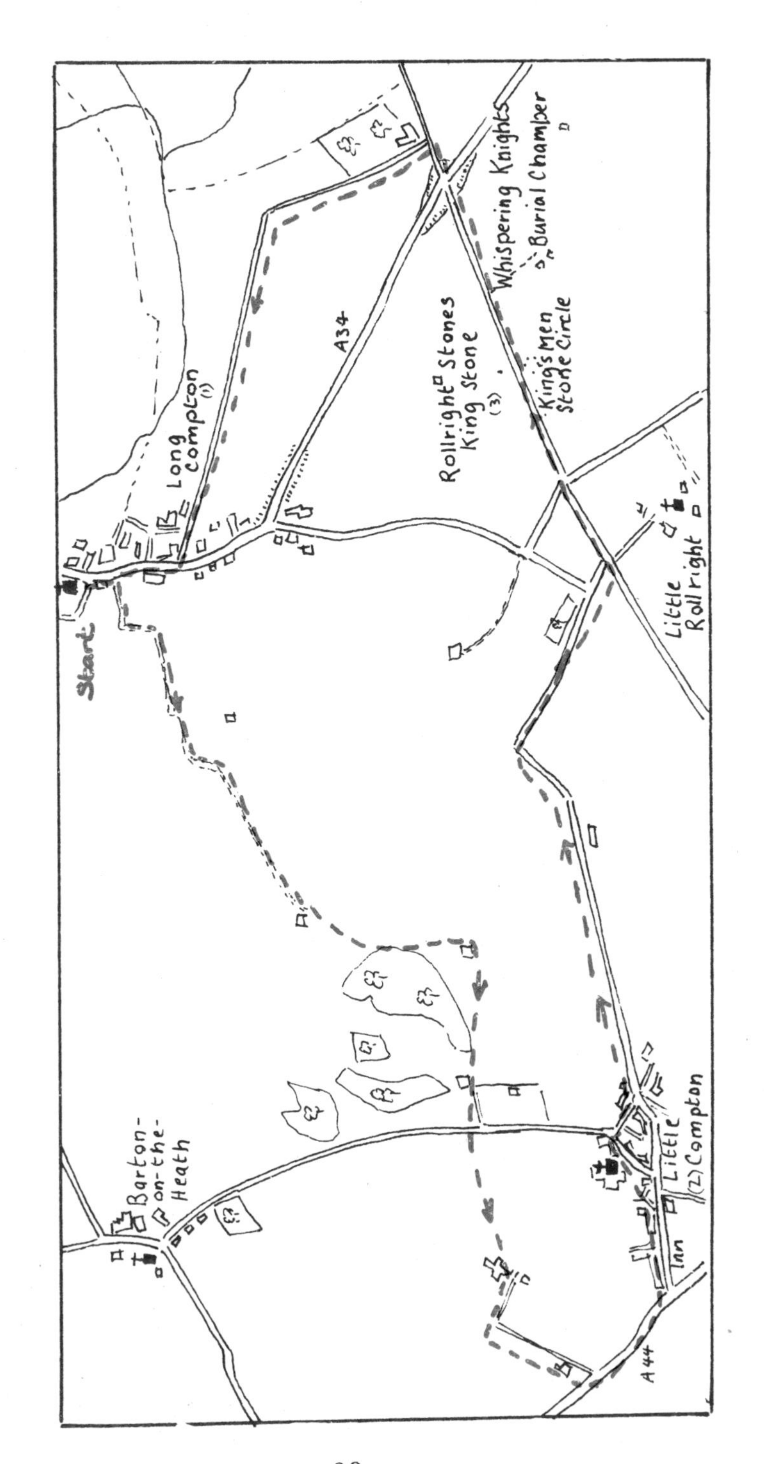
Start
Long Compton (1)
A34
Rollright Stones
King Stone (3)
King's Men Stone Circle
Whispering Knights
Burial Chamber
Little Rollright
Barton-on-the-Heath
Little (2) Compton
Inn
A44

This long but rewarding walk on the Warwickshire and Oxfordshire broders includes extensive views, the two handsome villages of Long Compton (1) and Little Compton (2), and a visit to the famous Rollright Stones (3). The going is varied, a pleasant ramble over pasture and arable in the morning, with a long gentle ascent up a quiet lane to the commanding ridge after lunch. Many footpaths round Little Rollright have disappeared under the corn belt, but the ancient ridge and furrow is still abundant near Little Compton.

Go left from the lane opposite the church, past the garage, Manor House and butcher's shop. Just beyond the Post Office on the right are the remains of an old market cross and fountain. Go right here, up a gravel farm drive, into a long open field with medieval strips still apparent, and a tall hedge on the right. The track swings left to a metal gate on the right, passes through, and continues straight ahead. Another swing to the left, another gate, another pasture. The track remains firm and well-defined, for this walk can be attempted in all weathers. It climbs gently under power lines past a group of farm buildings towards a wooded ridge and gate beneath a tall oak, with a spring called Rookham Well on the right. To the rear, Long Compton is spread out below, in front is Barton-on-the-Heath, and most impressively aligned on the right are the spires of Great Wolford and Todenham.

Through the gate a sunken lane lined with ash trees rises alongside a coppice to two large barns. This is Neakings, and the track goes sharp right to follow the hedge alongside arable fields. Ahead is a stone house and barn – Wheelbarrow Castle – and then a cross-roads with a wooden footpath sign. Go straight over and follow the hedge. In the valley on the left, Little Compton comes into sight. There are two more arable fields, and then in the right-hand corner of the second, under a tall ash, is an entry into a bridle-path leading left past a group of houses, over a cattle grid, and on to a lane which descends by Salter's Well Farm to the A44. Turn left past the garage, and left again to Little Compton and the excellent Red Lion with its local ales and tasty menu.

From the pub go left through the village and pause to admire the splendid Elizabethan manor. The church adjoining it has an ancient tower and an illustrative modern window. Continue up the road which bends left by a wall, and then right past a line of yews and young limes, opposite which stands solidly a long row of cottages. Now there is a steady climb to the hilltop quarry, where the lane bends first left, then right past a tall pylon concealed behind the hedge. Long Compton lies to the left in the valley pierced by the frenetic A34. The views are splendid up here and remain so all the way past a conifer coppice and a left turn to the village. Go straight on to the next junction, turn left, and come upon the Rollright Stones. Carry on to the crossing with the A34, over which is a lane. After about ¼ mile, another lane on the left leads steeply off the ridge down past Butlers Road Farm into the valley, turns left and returns arrow-straight to Long Compton.

(1) Long Compton is well-named, an attractive village of grey-brown stone houses which seems to stretch endlessly along the A34 at the bottom of a secluded valley. Unfortunately, like too many otherwise pleasant villages situated on a main road, it suffers from ceaseless traffic which ruins any chance of a leisurely reflective appraisal of its charms.

The church of St. Peter and St. Paul has a 13th century nave but has been rather heavily restored in the mid-Victorian period. Today it is chiefly noteworthy for the unusual lych-gate house dating from the late 16th century which was probably the priest's or sacristan's residence and more recently was used as a cobbler's shop. The churchyard has a large collection of close-clipped yew trees which, at a distance, resemble a cluster of huge green skittles.

On the village outskirts, there are still a number of tall hedgerows which divide the fields and give added interest to the patchwork of crops, meadows and pastures. There is also evidence of hedge grubbing and mechanical lopping which, if continued, will soon change the scene completely. One of the most attractive features of the English countryside is the hedgerow – particularly the thick quickset thorn hedges of the Midlands. When the common fields were enclosed in the late 18th century quickset hedges were planted to mark boundaries by cutting slips or quicks from the ancient thorn trees which were so plentiful everywhere. These were set alongside ditches and rooted in soil enriched with nutrients drained from the manured fields, and because they grew so quickly, formed excellent boundaries and created a splendid patchwork pattern all over the countryside. To break a quickset hedge was a serious felony but in the last two decades a staggering 100,000 miles of hedgerows have been grubbed up in the interests of intensive agriculture, and many more have been mutilated beyond recognition by flails and hedge-trimming machines. All this, combined with the virtual disappearance of the elms, has sadly changed the face of the country landscape.

(2) The chief glory of Little Compton is the stone-built Elizabethan manor house, once the home of William Juxon who, as Bishop of London, attended Charles I at his execution at Whitehall in 1649. With the Restoration of the Stuart line in 1660, Juxon was created Archbishop of Canterbury and officiated at the coronation of Charles II in Westminster Abbey.

The church next door was practically rebuilt in 1864 except for the impressive 14th century tower. In the south chapel, a modern window commemorates William Juxon; in one panel he appears at the last meeting of Charles with his children; in another attending the King on the scaffold; in another escorting the royal corpse to St. George's Chapel, Windsor; and in a fourth, rejecting the blandishments of the adulterous Charles II.

(3) The Stones, which date from the early Bronze Age, lie to the south of the road in a circle about 100 feet in diameter and are known as the King's Men, who according to legend, were turned into stone by a witch. The stones are all badly weathered and it is doubtful if the circle represents their original position. They may in fact be all that remains of a much larger circle. Just to the east are four upright stones and a fallen capstone which must once have formed the entrance to a dolmen or burial chamber. These stones, known as the 'Whispering Knights', were said to be a group of the King's officers who had withdrawn from the main body to plot against the King. Acorss the road to the north is the larger monolith known as the 'King's Stone', the King himself, who had gone forward at the behest of the witch to reconnoitre the valley.

The desolate scene, the forbidding stones and their brooding atmosphere may well have given rise to the stories of witches' covens meeting round Long Compton in the 17th and 18th centuries. Indeed as late as 1875 a Long Compton man killed a poor old woman with a pitchfork, claiming that he was doing the village a service by getting rid of a witch. Further, he claimed that "there were sixteen witches in Long Compton and he would kill them all" (J. Burman – 'Warwickshire Families and Houses', p. 70).

SWINBROOK – ASTHALL – SWINBROOK – WIDFORD

Distances, a.m. 2½ miles, p.m. 2 miles.
O.S. Map No. 163 (Cheltenham and Cirencester), 1:50,000
Start point and car parking on grass verge near junction with track coming up from Widford. Grid reference 274128.

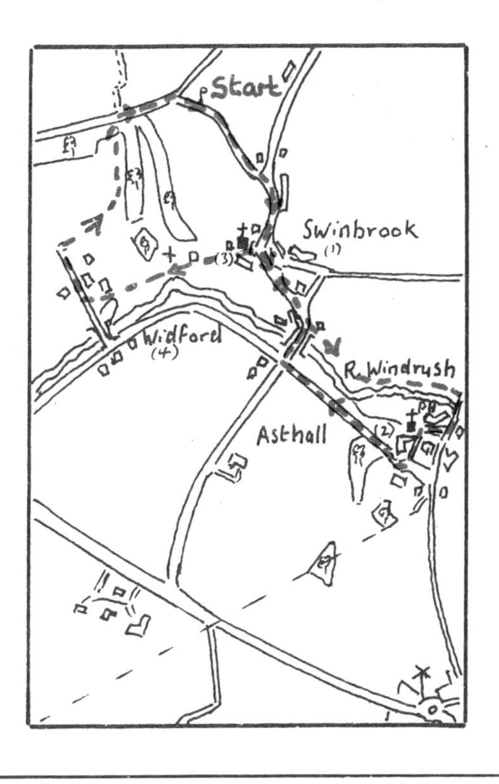

Quiet indeed is this part of Oxfordshire, and delightful the villages of grey stone and tiles. Our walk here is not strenuous, traversing coun-ry lanes and river pastures, with a slight climb at the end, but every tep abounds with interest for the lover of wild flowers, church archi-ecture and literary history.

Of all the colours that May displays, the most gaudy, and most old, is the un-English yellow of the oil-seed rape, great blotches of which mar the landscape at the start of the ramble, but soon along the ane to the right the whites and pinks of the cherries and pears mingle refreshingly with the varied greens of the burgeoning trees. In the hedgerows the bluebells stand erect among the cowparsley; the red campion is just showing, and nearer to the ground the lady smock, ground ivy and dead nettle add their delicate colouring to the scene. Colour of a different sort is provided by the fact that this is Mitford, or Redesdale, country (1).

The lane is flanked by a thin wall of dressed stone neatly laid, and leads gently right along the ridge. Large aircraft pass constantly overhead and presently at a wayside seat a gradual descent begins to Swinbrook past a cottage with tiny mauve toadflax adorning its walls. Turn to the right on the road and walk by a brook, then pass a large house with grey stone tiles over which martins are swooping. Over the brow is the church, to be visited later, then on the right a large pool which is home for several pairs of Canada geese.

The road twists and turns, and veers towards the 'Swan Inn'. Opposite it is a yellow marker at a stone stile. Climb over and, keeping the tall hedge on the right, walk towards a dead elm. The path gradually diverges from the Windrush, that river synonymous with the Cotswolds, and goes diagonally left across the grass to the field corner. Here is a double stile enclosing an upright boundary stone. A wood of every conceivable shade of green rises up on the left. The way traverses the lush meadow following the stone wall. Where this goes off to the left, the path wends half right towards two tall beeches not yet in leaf, and rejoins the river as it meanders in from the right.

Asthall manor and church are now clearly visible among the trees and a line of tall willows contrasts with a similar line of severely-pollarded stumps ahead. Across the next meadow and on the lane a bridge straddles the clear green depths of the Windrush. A curious feature of the right-hand parapet is a lower cut section with the representation of a rifle and bayonet incised in the stone, together with an indecipherable inscription. A separate channel, possibly to siphon off flood or drainage water, runs alongside the main river.

From this pleasant spot, the road continues in the direction of the village, passing on the corner a recently collapsed and newly repaired section of the dry stone wall overlooking a pond. The walls in this district are invariably neat and solid, having a preponderance of flattish stones similar in shape to the roof tiles, but slightly larger. The lane continues under horse chestnuts about to burst into bloom, straight on past the inviting and superbly named Maytime Inn to the church of

Asthall (2). It turns left past the churchyard and right past the entrance to the Manor, rises up a gently slope, and then descends, with the Windrush across a field on the right blazing with dandelions. Insignificant singly, in a mass these humble flowers form a brilliant carpet of deep yellow much warmer than the lurid metallic hue of the rape. The lane delights with its views of the river, inn, and Swinbrook church, then swings right past the cricket field and goes on to the Swan. The rural scene is perfect, and no expatriate's dream of home could be more vivid or evocative. The Swan proved to be well-named, for on a small island to the right of the bridge, one of these majestic creatures was sitting on her huge nest of reeds and, oblivious to all passers-by, was quietly building her platform still higher out of reach of imaginary floods while her cob preened himself nearby. Inside the ancient hostelry excellent refreshment can be enjoyed.

On leaving, turn left to Swinbrook church (3) past a barn and group of long-roofed buildings, and enter the churchard. Beyond the two Mitford graves near the porch is a small gate on the left with 'Path to St. Oswalds' written on it. This path, enclosed at first, leads through two fields to the tiny church of Widford, (4), now isolated, but once the focal point of a busy medieval village. A clear track, possibly the old village street, leads away from the church to a gate, passes through it, and goes uphill past the imposing house with the date 1696 inscribed on it. Follow the route upwards. Common wild flowers flourish on the wide verge out of reach of pesticides and sprays, but soon the gaudy rape comes into sight ahead, signalling the end of the walk. Where the track joins the lane turn right past a coppiced and waymarked footpath, walk up the little hill and return to the start point.

(1) Batsford was the original home of the Mitfords, but the wildly-eccentric family, known to us mainly through the literary and political activities of the six daughters, resided at Asthall Manor, then at Swinbrook House, a large rectangular stone residence built just outside the village for the Second Baron Redesdale, their titular head, and himself a man of extraordinary habits, language and principles. Jessica, in her book 'Hons. and Rebels', describes their peregrinations thus – "From Batsford Mansion to Asthall Manor to Swinbrook House to Old Mill Cottage' was our slogan to illustrate the decline of the family fortunes from Grandfather's day". Unity was an unrepentant Fascist, once on close terms with Hitler himself, and attempted suicide on the outbreak of war between England and Germany. Nancy became a writer and novelist of considerable distinction, and together with Unity is buried in Swinbrook churchyard. Tom, the only son and heir, died on army service in Burma in 1945, and is commemorated by a plaque on

the west wall, as is his father, who lived till 1958. Jessica, also a rebel against the restraints of her narrow – if indulgent – upbringing, preferred the hammer and sickle to the swastika, took part in the Spanish Civil War, and married another aristocratic rebel who was also to lose his life, this time in the R.A.F. Diana married Sir Oswald Mosley, leader of the British Blackshirts. Jessica's book describes in uproarious detail the childhood experiences of the girls as they grew up in the stifling atmosphere of the great houses of the 20s and 30s, and their highly individualistic reactions to their over-indulgent mother and outrageously quixotic father. "Hons." they were by birth, and "rebels" by nature, strange products of this most peaceful corner of England, and of the restrictive environment in which they passed their childhood.

(2) On the right of the churchyard path at Asthall is an interesting wool-bale tomb with a skull cut into the stone, and behind the church the gabled facade of the great Elizabethan house rises up to complete a delightful and impressive enclave. The church, together with those of Swinbrook and Widford must surely make up the most interesting trio in Oxfordshire. Dedicated to St. Nicholas, it was, until the end of the 19th century, in the patronage of Eton College and dates in part from the 12th century though it contains examples of the transitional style in its pillars, with Early English lancet windows in the north aisle and perpendicular ones in the south. In the north chapel is an effigy beneath a stone canopy of Lady Joan Cornwall, wife of King John's grandson, Edmund. She is dressed in wimple and robes. On the floor are the Bateman tombs, and nearby is an ancient stone altar, possibly unique in that is has a built-in piscina. The chancel has double sedilia, another piscina, and an aumbry to contain the sacrement. The wall paintings date from 1892, forming, with the roof and general fabric, part of the essential Victorian restoration which has preserved so many of our places of worship. The perpendicular tower completes a handsome and intimate building.

(3) In Swinbrook churchyard more examples of wool-bale tombs confront the visitor, together with a great perpendicular east window which lost most of its glass in 1940, shattered by German bombs. At least it now makes the 13th century chancel much lighter and illuminates the fascinating Fettiplace effigies, groups of figures set one above the other, reclining as if at a Roman banquet. Those outside the sanctuary, of Sir Edmund, his father and grandfather, are executed in rather stiff Tudor style, but those inside it, of a later Sir Edmund, his father, and uncle, are more life-like, and rendered in Stuart fashion. The seat of the Fettiplaces, who traced their descent from Anthony, esquire to Henry

VII in the early 16th century, was the original Swinbrook House destroyed in 1806, and they were, for three centuries, Lords of the Manor and patrons of St. Mary's church, which, like that at Asthall, dates from the 12th century. It has a clerestory – a sure sign of increasing prosperity – dating from the 15th century, and the misericords came from Burford Priory. It too has much to thank Victorian restoration for, and later the Redesdales, who presented the pews and chandeliers.

The living was in the gift of his Lordship who was in the habit of grilling hopeful applicants for the post in terrifying fashion, amusingly described by Jessica as she eavesdropped with one of her sisters from underneath the stairs. "None of those damn complicated foreign tunes", he would roar, "I'll give you a list – 'Holy, Holy, Holy', 'Rock of Ages', 'All things Bright and Beautiful' and the like". No sermon could take longer than ten minutes by stopwatch, after which there would be a signal to bring it to a close, and no Popish nonense like "Smells and Lace" (incense and choir robes). On the other hand, church attendance for the whole family, together with nannies, governesses and servants was rigorously enforced, rain or shine, accompanied by several dogs, a goat, a snake and a dove – the children's pets. These were either tethered or imprisoned in tombs with high railings and added their contributions to the singing within. Now, two of the family are buried here, and two more commemorated, in the precincts which they had honoured during their lifetimes in true Church of England fashion.

(4) 'Widford' means the 'Ford by the Willows', and indeed the ground is low-lying with large pools on the left. The church with its small bell turret, enclosed by stone walls against which the tall yellow wall rocket grows, was built by monks of St. Oswald's Priory, Gloucester, on the site of a Roman villa. Parts of the original tessellated flooring still lie exposed in the chancel. Perhaps the body of St. Oswald, King of Northumbria , killed in battle by Penda of Mercia in 642, rested here on its way to Gloucester for burial in the Priory, and the church was certainly in use until its parent house was dissolved, after which it declined with its village and fell into serious disrepair, to be restored by public subscription in 1904. It still contains ancient treasures like the 13th century tub-shaped font, has Jacobean altar rails and 18th century box pews, and in its general appearance proclaims its 12th century origin. Once again the double sedilia, piscina and aumbry bear silent witness to former constant usage, and the medieval wall paintings express the frail mortality of man much more vividly than any words of priest or prior.

WALK 10

WROXALL – BADDESLEY CLINTON – ROWINGTON – WROXALL

Distances, a.m. 4 miles, p.m. 3 miles.
O.S. Map No. 139 (Birmingham), 1:50,000.
Start point and car parking in lane behind Wroxall Village School. Grid reference 225714. Please do not inconvenience school or local residents.

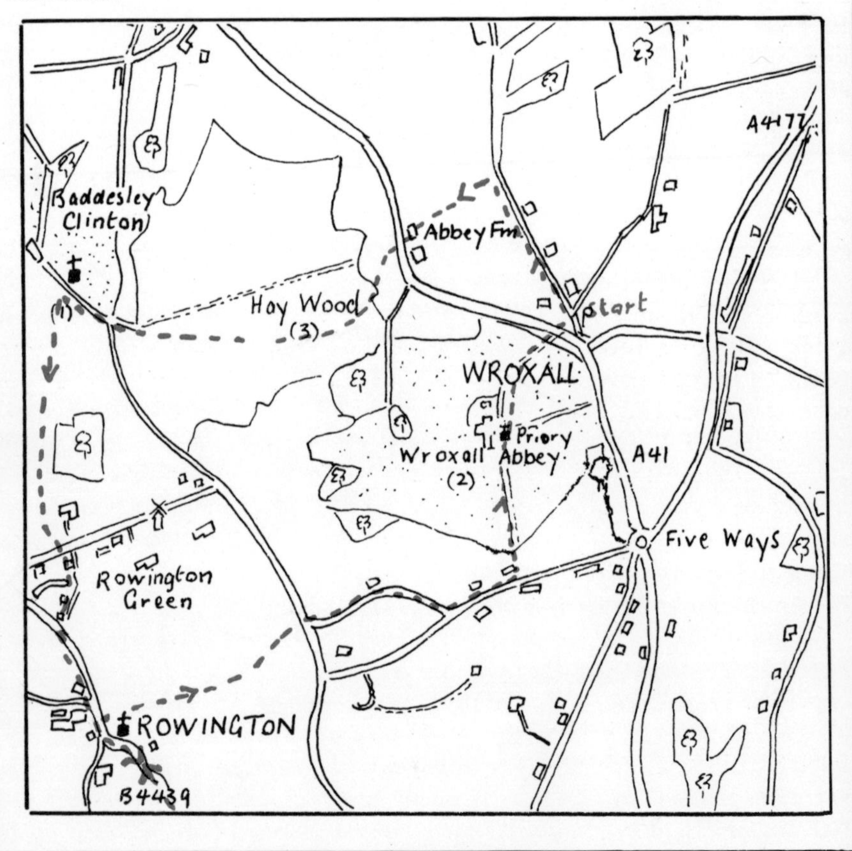

This is a varied walk, flat, comprising a morning visit to St. Michael's church, Baddesley Clinton (1), a glimpse of the famous moated manor now in the care of the National Trust, and an afternoon saunter through the parkland of Wroxall Abbey (2). The going is a mixture of pasture, woodland and arable, which can be muddy in winter.

Start by walking down the lane away from the houses beneath a line of chestmuts and past a lych-gate and cemetery. On the left stands Abbey Farm, and a field gate soon gives access to two fields on this side where the path hugs the hedge making straight for a farm gate with a blue marker. Go through it, swing left and then right through the farm buildings to come to the A41. Turn left along the wall, and cross the busy road to a lane on the corner with a sign 'Wood Corner House'. Go up it to the half-timbered house, follow the road left and at once turn right through the barns and go through a double green metal gate into the field. Hay Wood can now be seen ahead, so skirting the hedge on the right and ignoring the noisy but securely-enclosed German shepherd dogs, make for a small gate in the corner, enter the wood, and turn left up the ride.

The walking through the trees is peaceful, and after 20 minutes without deviating from the track Old Keeper's Lodge is reached at a wide gate. Go on to a lane, cross it, and continue up the tree-lined approach to St. Michael's churchyard. Just before the gate, take the path on the left bordered by a wire fence and giving a side view of Baddesley Clinton House. It leads through two gates, up the side of an arable field to a short lane alongside a wood. Primroses grow here in spring. A muddy gateway leads to a track between a hedge and a wire fence to Lyons Farm and its herd of beautiful Jerseys, then to the road at Rowington Green. Straight over alongside the cricket ground is Queen's Drive which soon joins the B 4439. Follow this to the left past the school, now closed, and then the fine Norman church of St. Lawrence on its dominant hill. Descend the busy road with care for about ½ mile with the huge canal embankment on the right, an impressive monument to pick and shovel engineering, and arrive at the Cock Horse Inn, its name evocative, its food and drink excellent.

Return to the church. Find a path on the right leading down and out of the churchyard at the bottom. Make for the field corner and stile, then follow the right side of the pasture to an arable field. Cross this diagonally to a stream. Over it, bear hard left along the edge of the field following the markers, turn right in the corner, and half way along the hedge look for a small plank bridge and stile on the left. Cross it, keep to the left again and make for a stile at a lane near a junction of roads. Take the left-hand fork uphill past Mouseley Hill Farm. The sunken lane leads to another junction. Go left, up Case Lane past houses and Moat Farm, noticing the tall chimneys of Wroxall Abbey on the left. Just before the quaintly-named Case is Altered inn, a waymarked path goes over a stile on the left and leads across the field to another stile opposite. This one gives access to the wooded park. Keep straight on, with a belt of trees on the left, to a small gate ahead into the grounds. With the wall on the left, continue past the main entrance and a large pool to an iron gate. Leave the grounds through it and re-enter the park. Ahead across the grassland is an estate road going right to the A41 and the village school.

(1) The church is in a most secluded spot, beautiful in any season, but never more than in spring when the churchyard is a mass of snowdrops, primroses and daffodils. "Only on the Sabbath are signs of life seen here, and then but for a brief space", said John Hannett in his book 'The Forest of Arden' in 1863. Tranquil it is, save when the nearby manor house is open. St. Michael's – or St. James's as it was first dedicated according to a tablet on the wall – is not mentioned in Domesday and probably owes its origin to the powerful Norman family of de Clinton, the first holders of the manor in the early 14th century. As you enter, look for the memorial tablet set in the floor just inside the door to "Nicholas Brome 1517". The Bromes had bought the manor of Baddesley in 1438 and Nicholas, a vengeful son and jealous husband had committed a double mortal sin in slaying his father's murderer and later the parish priest of Baddesley whom he had found "chockinge my wife under ye chinne" in the parlour of the manor house. His remorse is clear from a passage in his will in which he bequeathed: "My soule unto Almighty God – and my body to be buried within the church of St. James, there as people may tread upon me when they come into the church" – and here indeed his remains were discovered when the church was restored in 1872.

The small nave and chancel contain a massive oak chest of early date, an early Norman font, and a beautiful east window of ten lights and intricate tracery. In the chancel is the decorated tomb of Sir Edward Ferrers and his wife, and on the floor a black granite tablet commemorates the twelve generations of Ferrers buried beneath, including the well-known Henry the 'Antiquary' who was Lord of the Manor for 70 years. Nicholas Brome's daughter married into the Ferrers family and thus started a dynasty whose direct male line died out in 1884 with the death of Marmion Ferrers. The nearby house was then sold in 1939, and after a thorough restoration of the fabric, the new owners took the name of Ferrers, ensuring the survival of both house and name until the building was transferred to the National Trust in 1980. It is but a stone's throw from the church down an avenue of trees, and whilst a short diversion from the walk permits a glimpse of the "perfect late medieval manor house" (Pevsner), a full visit is to be recommended.

(2) The majestic trees and carefully-maintained lawns and shrubs of Wroxall Abbey, now a school for girls, can be admired from the path running alongside its walls. It started life as a Priory whose scanty remains, consisting of two roofless ruins of ashlar blocks, still lie among the trees. It was founded in 1141 by a certain Richard, Lord of the Manor of Hatton, who gave the nuns all the land of Wroxall. The Prioress thus became a considerable land owner, having at one time a Sir Edward Ferrers of Baddesley as her steward and a Richard Shakespeare as her bailiff. At Dissolution, Henry VIII conveyed the estates to Robert Burgoyne, who pulled down the religious house and erected a manor comprising two half-timbered wings and a hall block. This remained in the possession of the Burgoynes until 1713 when Sir Christopher Wren bought it for £19,600, though as he died in 1723, he did not enjoy much personal contact with it. However, his descendants did, and in 1812, Christopher Roberts Wren, after service in India, restored the parish church of St. Leonards, now standing in private ground within the school gates, and 'modernised' the house. He dies in 1828 and the estate, wooded and park-like as it is today, was sold in 1861 to James Dugdale who demolished the old house and built the present one.

There is a mystery here – the village of Wroxall was certainly emparked, as the ridge and furrow on the north-west slopes near the house indicates, especially under snow. But when did this take place? and where exactly was the village? Probably grouped around the church, whose status with regard to the few remaining villagers today is anomalous. It stands within the grounds of the school, and whilst parishioners are welcome to services there it is used mainly by the girls. It contains memorials to the Wren family and some notable stained glass, and can be visited with prior permission from the school bursar. The grounds of the Abbey are open to the public at certain times during the summer but otherwise they are private. From the small iron gate the quiet beauty of the place can best be appreciated. A flock of Canada geese has taken possession of the pond on the right at breeding time, and on the left stands a magnificent avenue of oaks leading to a tall wrought-iron grille giving entry to the grounds. The high estate walls bulge outwards in a series of crescent-shaped curves designed as sun traps, and the peaceful walk down the estate road forms a fitting end to the day.

WALK 11

ASTON CANTLOW – NEWNHAM – WILMCOTE – ASTON CANTLOW

Distances, a.m. 3 miles, p.m. 3½ miles.
O.S. Map no. 151 (Stratford-upon-Avon), 1:50,000.
Start point Aston Cantlow village. Grid reference 138599.

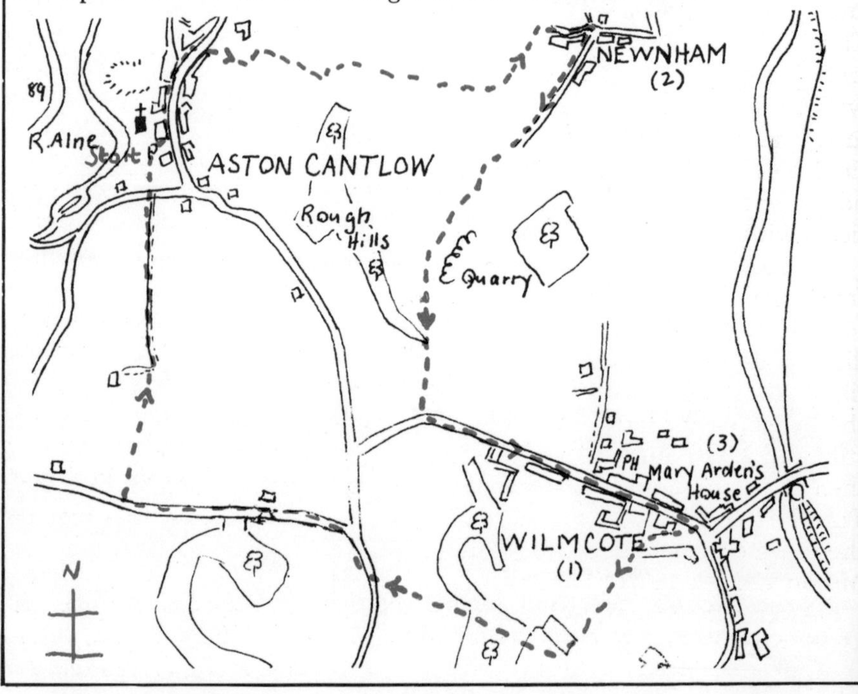

Here is a walk over pasture and arable, with a short stretch of road before lunch at Wilmcote (1). A gently-rising route over the Rough Hills takes us through the isolated hamlet of Newnham (2), and past the disused lias stone quarries. An interesting feature of the afternoon walk is the stretch of path, deep with bark chips, forming a horse gallop, just outside Wilmcote. This affords good springy footing, contrasting with some damp woodland later.

Park with prior permission, either behind the Kings Head or opposite the Working Men's Club in Guild Road. Turn left from the former, or right from the latter, up the village street past Castle Farm and the telephone box on the left. This is Bearley Road, and at the last house a footpath sign points right. The track goes through arable fields and under power lines to an ash tree by a ditch. Go left, then right and keeping the hedge on the left, pass another ash tree. Turn half left and start climbing a path between hawthorn hedges and dog roses. These are the Rough Hills from which there is a good view of the village of Aston Cantlow. Sloes and elderflowers are abundant.

At the top the track goes straight on with the hedge on the left, alongisde more arable, through a gateway and donwhill through a pasture to an iron gate near a ditch. Swing left beneath a line of ash trees past a tin shack. The well-made track now leads straight to Newnham and continues past a long low gabled house to Lower Farm on the right. Then it turns left past the old village green opposite a huge chestnut tree in a garden. Turn right down the lane by a small red building and walk under the young chestnut trees on the left. Weeping willows grow in the garden on the right. Look for an old iron pump on its own in a field on the left. Next on the same side are some farm buildings and a house where the track, half concrete, goes straight on alongside wheat fields with the hedge on the left. It can be very muddy here.

A stone water trough marks the entrance to the second field. The track goes directly ahead, but at the top of the field swings right and soon left. Behind the tall hawthorn hedges are the extensive but long disused quarries which were once an important economic element for the district. The grassy track now passes through an iron gate, still with the hedge on the left, to the field corner where a narrow path leads to a stile and a gate into the next field, with the hedge now on the right. It then descends along what was once a hedge line to a gate by the road. Turn left and walk up the hill to Wilmcote passing modern housing and then some substantial stone cottages on the left, and arrive at the Mason's Arms, an excellent pub.

After refreshment, walk on in the same direction past an old chapel. Mary Arden's House (3) is just down the road to the left, the Swan House Hotel is on the right. Near the roadside sign "Swanfold" a road goes to the right through a bungalow estate. Find No. 25 and go up the narrow entry on its right. Turn left and walk up the horse gallop. The ground rises to a hedge with a stile in the left-hand corner near a privet bush. Cross into the field and walk along the right boundary over clumps of diminutive scarlet pimpernel growing between the corn and the field edge. The path goes left, then right past a wired-off area to the field corner. Turn right out of the field, then left to face a metal gate. Do not go through the gate, but turn left down a grassy track for about 200 yards to another gate on the left.

Here follow the path on the right as it wanders through the wood – it is cut up badly by horses' hooves and can be wet, but goes pleasantly downhill widening into an ash glade. It passes through clumps of dog roses and tall vetches, and then gradually climbs by a field edge to a road. Here, take a right turn and continue to a junction (not far), where, take the left fork for Haselor and Great Alne. Pass the drive on the left leading to the sombre-looking Woodside, past clumps of blue cranesbill blooming amid the grasses. A red barn appears on the right, then the wood on the left sweeps down to the roadside. About 300 yards further on, high up in the hedgerow a footpath sign appears, pointing right. The stile is awkward, but not the going, which is easy now along the left-hand border of huge cereal fields, with Aston Cantlow church clearly in sight, and a long-ruined barn on the left. A farm track soon leads directly to a lane, across which is a stile. The final stretch is straight across the meadow to a foot-bridge by a willow, where the path leads past the rear of the old schoolhouse and the churchyard to the lych gate and the Kings Head.

" There is nothing which has yet been contrived
by man by which so much happiness is produced
as by a good tavern or inn."

Samuel Johnson

King's Head Inn, Aston Cantlow

Aston Cantlow, originally Estone Cantelupe, sprawls north and south along the Wootton Wawen – Billesley road where it widens into a small green. The village owes its unusual name to William Cantelupe, a Norman lord who was granted the Manor by King John in 1205. One of this family became Bishop of Hereford in 1215 and was canonised as St. Thomas. The Cantelupe castle built close to the river Alne behind Castle Farm had already fallen into decay by the end of the 14th century, and today nothing remains apart from some rough earthworks and a ditch. The economic growth of the village was equally short-lived, for although William de Cantelupe obtained grant of a market and fair in 1227, there is no subsequent mention of either. By the end of the 13th century there were four other markets and fairs – at Stratford, Bidford, Alcester and Henley-in-Arden – all within five miles of Aston Cantlow, and all on good roads built by the Romans.

Nevertheless, a guild survived in Aston Cantlow, was licensed in 1469, and the fine half-timbered building opposite the King's Head was erected as the Guild Hall in the 16th century. Its upper floor was used for manor courts up to 1770 and it is still performing a useful function for the village, as is the equally ancient King's Head.

The church of St. John the Baptist is largely 13th century, partly restored in the 19th century, and it is claimed that in this church in 1557 John Shakespeare married Mary Arden, the daughter of a yeoman farmer from Wilmcote, though there is no ecclesiastical record of this event, the fruit of which was the birth of the great dramatist. The couple, it is also claimed, celebrated their wedding breakfast in the King's Head next door, where countless couples since then have enjoyed the famous duck suppers provided by this excellent inn. He came from Snitterfield, she from Wilmcote, then in the parish of Aston Cantlow, so the claim may well have foundation.

Together with the Rectory and the old schoolhouse, the church forms an attractive enclave. The great east window is in the flamboyant style and sets off the sturdy 13th century tower at the west end. There are three more in the south chancel wall, but those in the south nave wall are modern Gothic as this part was rebuilt in 1850. Inside is the restored chancel arch, framing the modern glass in the east window, where St. Thomas is depicted in the right-hand corner. There is also a 15th century font and pulpit and three fine old chests, the latter in the vestry beneath the tower.

(1) Wilmcote, except for its modern developments, is built mainly in 18th and 19th century brick and stone. The sturdy stone cottages passed on entering the village from the Aston road, date from the time of the opening of the local lime and cement works in 1830. The Masons'

Arms is another solidly built house of local materials, with its sign bearing the motto "Deus Dux" (God my Leader) proclaiming the presence of stone masons in the village.

(2) Newnham is now an isolated hamlet, consisting of two farms and some attendant cottages converted into modernised dwellings. It had a fairly large population when the quarries were in operation, and there were many more cottages, as is evidenced by the presence of a long, flat site, formerly occupied by a row of dwellings similar to those still standing, but now converted. The quarries were clearly extensive in their day, and stone from Newnham was used to repair the Clopton bridge at Stratford in 1541, (Accounts of Stratford Corporation – iii, 58n), whilst Wilmcote stone was employed in the building of St. Mary's church, Warwick after the great fire of 1694 (Churches of Warwickshire – 134n).

(3) Mary Arden's House, now owned by the Shakespeare Birthplace Trust and open to the public, is a great timber-framed structure, two-storied and rectangular, dating from the early 16th century. It is basically a hall house with dormers and open timbered ceilings, with huge, rough, low beams. The rooms are furnished in the heavy oak style of the period. Mary Arden was the youngest of eight daughters, and though the extensive farm buildings at the rear bear evidence of considerable prosperity, the finding of eight dowries must have imposed a continuous strain on the parental purse.

These buildings now house a collection of carts and agricultural implements formerly used in the district, but they were once given over th the manifold uses of medieval farming – wool, stores, brew houses and malting sheds, stables, calf-houses and piggeries, barns and butteries. A surviving reminder of those busy days is the nearby dovecot with its hundreds of nesting niches – an important source of winter meat.

WALK 12

WELFORD-ON-AVON – BARTON – BIDFORD – DORSINGTON – WELFORD-ON-AVON

Distances, a.m. 3½ miles, p.m. 4 miles from Barton, 4½ miles from Bidford. O.S. Map No. 151 (Stratford-upon-Avon) 1:50,000.
Start point Welford-on-Avon church. Grid reference 146522

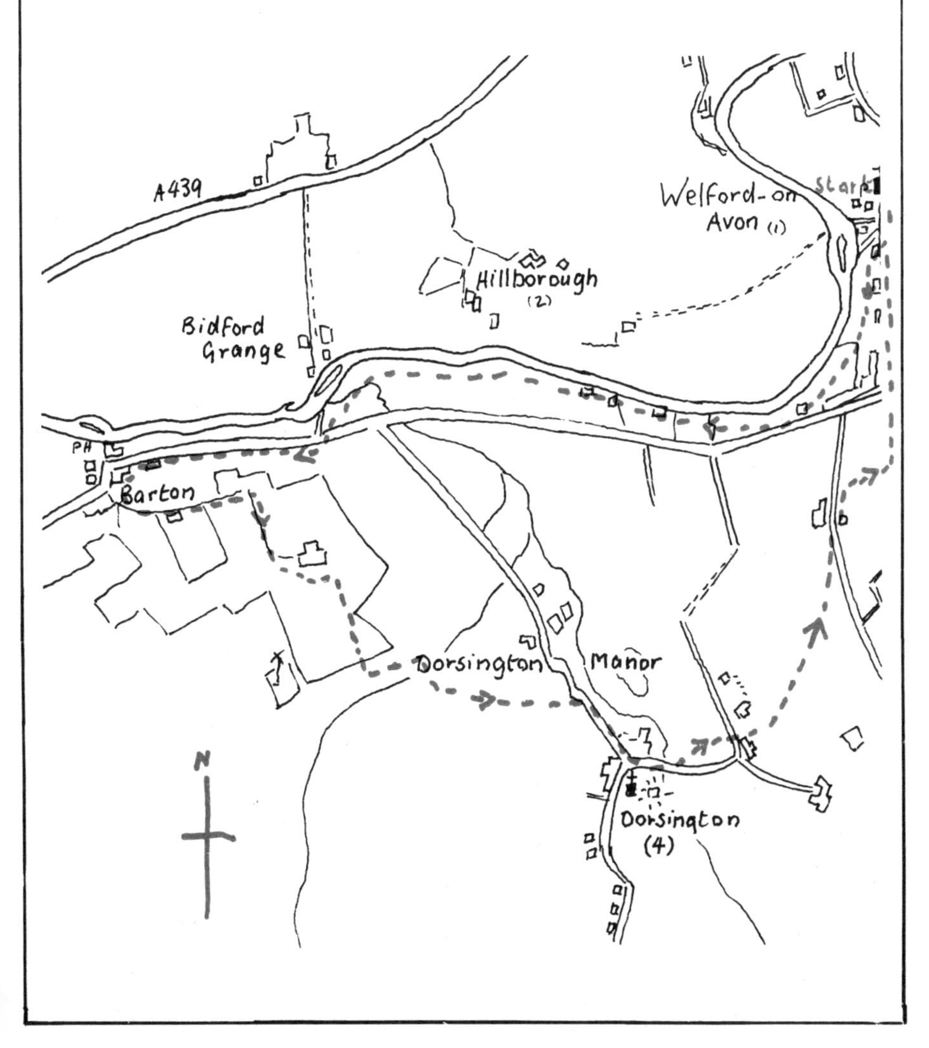

Flowering villages, riverside meadows, apple orchards and sheep pastures, with not a hill on the whole route – such is the background to this walk from Welford (1).

Park in Church Lane on the grass opposite 'Cleavers', a handsome Georgian residence, with the Norman church on the left. Turn right past the thatched cottages down Boat Lane, and when you hear the sound of a weir, look for a narrow path on the left which leads past the Mill House and the old mill itself, once essential to the village economy. Hereabouts was the ford which gave the place its name. Emerge on to the road, go left then right following a green arrowed sign through a caravan site. In the bottom right-hand corner climb a stile to the riverside path, sometimes muddy and slippery, but well-defined, leading now through glades of close blackthorn, now through groups of unpollarded willows, and finally across lush meadows frequented by flocks. All the way the Avon, host to moorhen and mallard, flows quietly alongside; the going is flat and easy, and soon on the other bank rise the tall Elizabethan chimneys of lonely West Hillborough Farm (2).

At the end of the long meadow is a green fishing hut just before a lock and weir. The river, broader here, becomes briefly turbulent, but soon has its force blunted by a long, debris-strewn island. Continue along the edge of a ploughed field and look for an imposing residence on the right bank. Here, swing left at the field corner, and cross a plank bridge over a small stream frequented by herons. Take the willow-lined track on the left up to the road, and turn right along the blackthorn hedge to Barton, past the flood signs and a static caravan site.

It is a pleasant hamlet with, on the left, a typical Cotswold manor house in lias stone, bearing an entablature 'John Paxton A.D. 1603' above its mullioned windows. On the right are some neat houses backing on to the river, and ahead the Cottage of Content, a welcoming inn serving good food and ale. The inn is of brick, but has 17th century timber-framing. Here the good folk of Birmingham and district from the caravan site mingle happily with the locals. The choice now is to lunch here or to press on to Bidford. Those opting for the latter will find the path behind the inn going left by yet another weir, stirring the Avon to temporary wrath. Cross the fields towards the town's ancient and historic bridge(3).

Retrace steps to Barton and where the road winds left and then right, in the left corner, take the clear track leading up between the tall hedgerows. Soon three dead elms appear on the left, and apple orchards, shielded by the hedges. Presently you come into open country and walk past three large Nissen-type huts on the right. Here, look back on Bidford, whose church bells now ring out across the intimate countryside on this Sunday morning.

In the onion fields grow masses of speedwell and dead nettle. Where the track swings right, observe the Cotswold Edge in the distance on that side, and catch a last glimpse of the Avon away on the left. Here are the orchards again, with chaffinches colonising the hedges, and larks rising. The track now goes left towards a farm, and the avenues between the apple trees are ablaze with dandelions. Outside the farmhouse are three old ploughs, a cart wheel in the gate, and nearby, several Morris Minors in various stages of undress. Past the house, turn immediately right where there is a huge pile of logs, then keep half-left towards another tall hedge with the well-pruned fruit trees now on the left. Walk with the hedge on the right, straight ahead to the end of the orchard. If you have timed your walk right, you will be amid a sea of blossom; otherwise you might be knee-deep in mud and water. Keep going to the gap at the bottom of the orchard. Look left and pick out two more hedge-gaps ahead across the arable.

Leave the orchard now and make for the second hedge-gap, noticing the yellow waymarkers on the left. At the gap, go right, and keeping the low hedge on the right, make straight for the bottom right-hand corner, where you will find a small bridge by a brick structure. Here a rutted track crosses at right-angles; follow it for a few yards, then go right, and keeping the hedge on the right, pick your way above, or alongside the tractor tracks. Go on until a group of buildings comes into sight on the left, and at the end of the next field, make for a white gate giving access to a lane, with Dorsington Manor Gardens away to the left. Go right along the road to Dorsington (4).

The way swings left, then right past more white gates, and after about ½ mile comes out on to the village green. Here go left with the church on the right and 'Aberfoyle', a black and white house on the left. Almost opposite the Moat House, look for a stile on the left by a white gate, metal this time. Go over the meadow to the wooden fence ahead, usually patrolled by a group of ponies, then turn right and walk along-side to a bridge over a brook. Go straight across the meadow ahead to a lane, with a black and white farm to the left, and a modern bungalow in front. This is Braggington, and the route is waymarked with wooden posts. Cross the lane into a low-lying and rather marshy field with a large farm building on the left, and make for the top left-hand corner where there are two stiles. Cross them, turn right, and keeping the hedge on that side, commence a gradual climb through four fields and over four stiles, all of them in the right-hand corners. The third field is a long one, and the fourth is ridge and furrow. Pause for breath at the top where the farm track crosses at right-angles, and look back on Bredon Hill – seldom out of sight in the Avon valley, except when wearing its hat.

Turn left through the gate and follow the track through the farm buildings. The route now becomes a metalled road and descends gently past a modern house on the right with a line of damson trees and telephone wires on the left. Where the trees end, and on the right, is a metal gate with a white marker on a circular green background. Go through the gate and across the field diagonally left, to a willow in the left-hand top corner, where a stile admits to the next meadow. Ahead is another stile, and a long field, rough and full of docks and thistles. Cross to Headland Road, and go straight along it past the school to Welford church and journey's end.

(1) The main street at Welford with its famous maypole, belies the ture character of the place. It speaks of modern affluence, but the original village is grouped around the church of St. Peter which is well worth a visit. Its comparative small size suggests that the medieval village had far fewer inhabitants than its modern counterpart. Approach the church from the lych gate, an exact modern replica of the original made at the end of the 14th century. The main doorway is decorated in chevrons, and inside are solid rounded arches, a Saxon font resting on small pillars, a 13th century parish chest, and a fine 17th century oak octagonal pulpit. The large east window by Christopher Webb dates from the 1920s, but blends well with the perpendicular side windows of the chancel.

The parish originally belonged to the Priory of Deerhurst, which was in turn a dependency of the French Abbey of St. Denis. Deerhurst monks built the original church at Welford, but during the 14th century, in the course of the Hundred Years War, the parish was taken from its French owners and given to the Abbey of Tewkesbury, though later is was to pass briefly into the ownership of Eton College. However, in 1441, Henry VI returned it to Tewkesbury Abbey once more and the monks did a good deal of improving work, installing the present aisle windows and decorating them on the outside with the head of the King and his wife, Margaret of Anjou. Today, the bell-ringers of St. Peter's, Welford-on-Avon have a fair reputation for their skill.

(2) Viewed from across the river, the house and its cluster of low, red-tiled barns certainly looks stark, even forbidding on a stormy day, and though the alliteration trips easily off the tongue, the title of "Haunted Hillborough" is understandable. The village suffered from plague and enclosures, became deserted, and the present houses were built largely from the abandoned stones. The ghost that supposedly haunts the great house near the farm, has variously been described as a White lady, Anne Whately, in love with Shakespeare, who pined away when he married Anne Hathaway; a screaming man, an unfortunate shepherd, stoned by his fellows for some unspeakable crime; Polly, a wronged Victorian servant maid, and a ghostly rider or coach crossing the fields.

(3) There must have been a ford at Bidford-on-Avon from time immemorial. The Roman Ryknield or Icknield Street ran north/south on its way from Alcester to Chipping Campden, and crossed the river by a ford just east of the church. A bridge was built about 200 yards further down the river in the 15th century, mainly from the stone of the dissolved Alcester Priory. It has eight arches which today show signs of frequent repair. Its importance as a crossing is indicated by the

fact that in 1449, John Carpenter, Bishop of Worcester, offered a year's indulgences to all who would help repair it.

The bridge was broken by Charles I in 1644 in an attempt to cover his rear during his march from Worcester to Oxford, and repaired again in 1650. Its arches are segmental and pointed and the cut-waters still sturdily divide the stream as it flows evenly beneath the traveller standing above. With the building of its by-pass, Bidford has at last found peace from the noise, dirt and fumes of traffic, but it was not always so in Shakespeare's time, for the bard is reputed to have engaged in toping contests with his friends against the locals, and to have come off second best – hence the appellation "Drunken Bidford". These contests took place in the Falcon in the High Street, just off the small market place, an L-shaped, 16th century house, with mullioned windows protected by dripstones and string courses. It is no longer a place of refreshment, but there are plenty of others to choose from. The church of St. Lawrence has a 13th century nave and chancel, but so much work was done by the Victorian restorers in adding side aisles, that it is almost impossible to envisage its original form.

(4) Dorsington Manor Gardens have much of interest for nature lovers and those who like domestic fowl and duck. There is a tea shop and the usual tourist paraphernalia, but the real importance of the place is in the concern shown for the survival of rare breeds which are on display in open pens, and it is especially fascinating in the spring to see the chicks being reared in the stable block.

Dorsington village is a mixture of old and new, all neat and well-tended, with a rather incongruous red-brick church. In spring, the village opens its gardens to the public under the National Gardens Scheme for charitable purposes, and the little church plays its part in this worthy activity. Kathleen and May, two village ladies who were busy burnishing the brasses and spring-cleaning the church interior, had much to tell about the church and about village life. The original St. Peter's was burned down in 1753, rebuilt by public subscription, and re-opened in 1870, the living being combined with Pebworth and Honeybourne. There is a plaque to this effect on the north wall, and some attractive stained glass windows on the same side, dedicated to St. Cecilia and St. Margaret. St. Peter and St. Paul preside over the south wall. A combined lectern and pulpit in oak stands near the minute choir stalls, and all is tended with an almost tangible love and care. In the churchyard are eight conical shaped yew trees, presumably planted at the opening of the "new" church, as well as the almost statutory ancient yew which must have survived the fire.

Kathleen and May spoke of the village community spirit exemplified by an autumn "walkabout", when most houses display produce stalls and serve teas, the proceeds going to church funds. A final mystery was cleared up when they explained the presence of a moat, now dry, surrounding nearby Moat House. Apparently in former days the house was the resting place of the Bishop of Gloucester in his progress round his scattered diocese.

WALK 13

ALCESTER–WIXFORD–EXHALL–OVERSLEY GREEN–ALCESTER

Distance 5½ miles. O.S. Map No. 150 (Worcester & the Malverns) 1:50,000.
Start point, free car park in School Road at top of Henley Street.
Grid reference 091575.

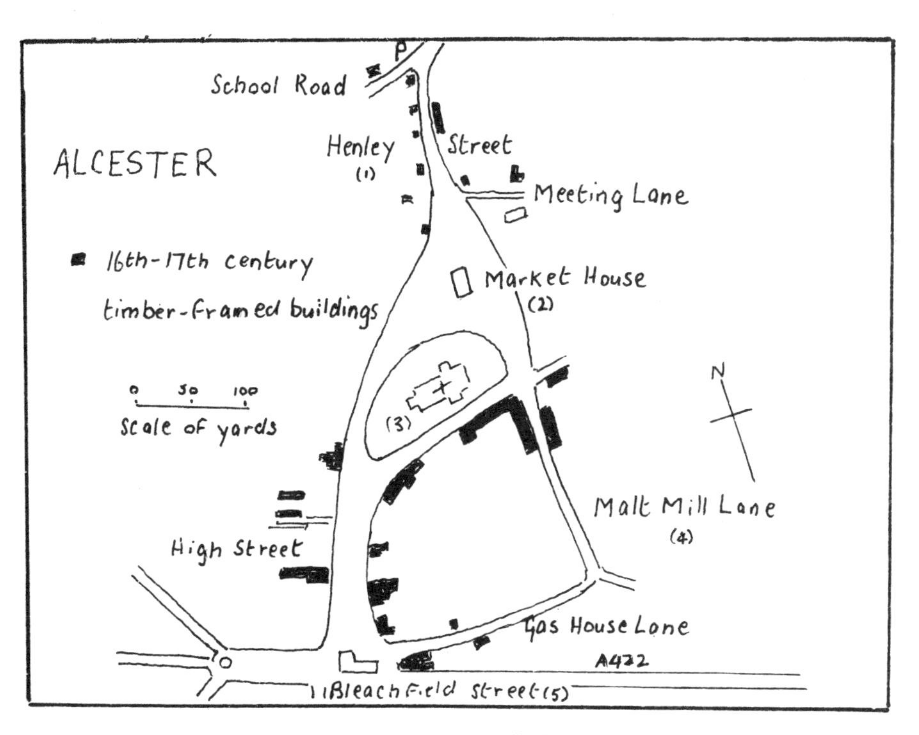

The walk begins with a leisurely stroll through the heart of Alcester, down Henley Street (1), past the Market House (2), and church (3). Go down Malt Mill Lane (4) to the left of the church. At the end is Gas House Lane which emerges on to the A422 near the Swan Hotel. Here, turn left down Bleachfield Street (5), which ends in an unmade track crossing the river Arrow. Pass through a caravan site and turn right into a lane. At the first bend, go over a stone stile on the left and walk along the side of a field with the hedge on the left. To the right on a gentle slope is Ragley Hall (6), and below it on the riverside, is ancient Arrow Mill (7).

The track, following the Roman Ryknield Street, now climbs through a spinney to a junction of farm tracks near a Dutch barn. Go left and climb gradually towards the dominant mound where Oversley Castle once stood.

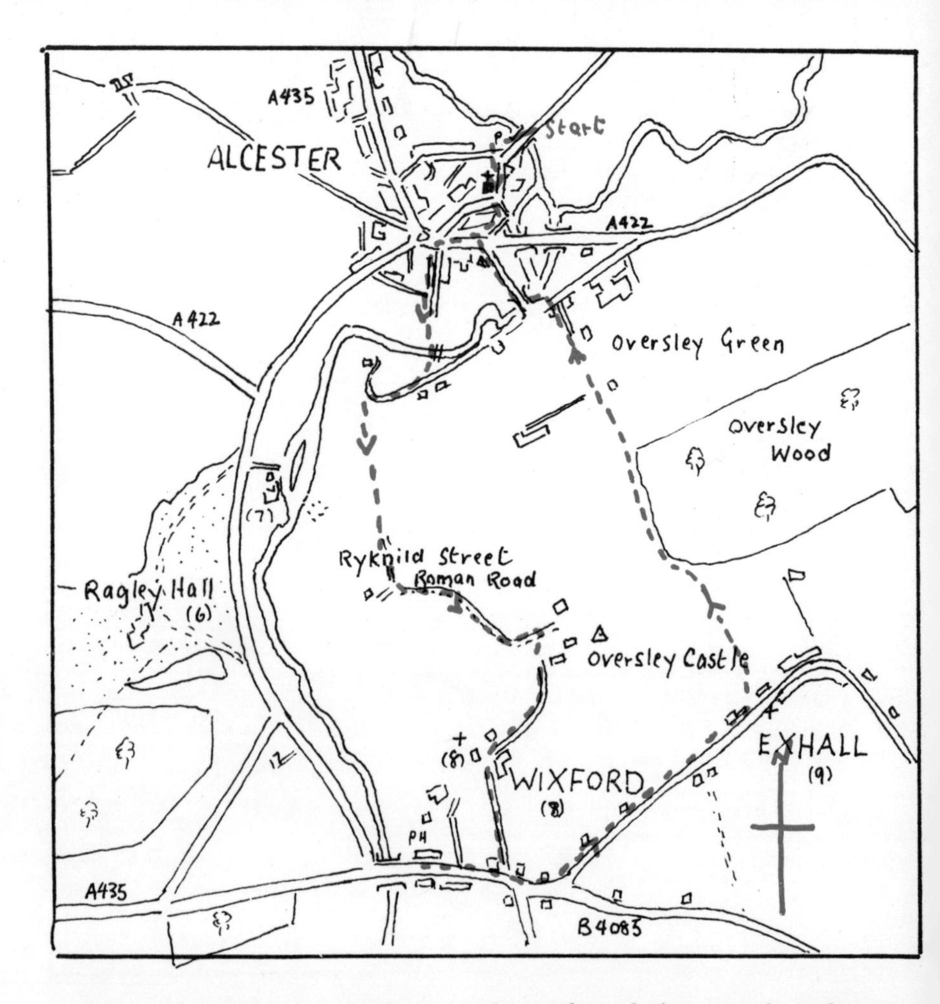

The oak-crowned summit now the realm of sheep and rook, commands extensive all-round views. The way swings right, goes up, and then downwards through an avenue of chestnut, birch, poplar and laburnum, whose brilliant yellow blossoms, falling in cascades from the branches, accompany us all the way to Wixford church (8).

Continue to the left to the B4085, then turn right through the village to the Fish Inn by the river. Shakespeare once drank here it is budiously claimed. The food, drink and surroundings are nevertheless very good. After lunch, retrace steps to the Three Horseshoes at the road junction; proceed left and left again to come by a narrow lane to Exhall (9). The church is on the right; on the left the village notice board and a footpath sign pointing up the cricket field and a hilly sheep pasture. Climb to a couple of fence-stiles in the right hand corner. Walk along the arable field with the hedge on the right and the mound of Oversley Castle standing out boldly on the left.

At a junction of tracks, continue straight ahead to a bridle path much churned up by horses, and skirting Oversley Wood. This soon emerges among the houses of Oversley Green, becomes a road, and at some neat, thatched cottages, swings right, then left, to cross the river Alne by a bridge built in 1600. Over the busy A422 are a green and a path leading to the bottom of Malt Mill Lane.

Alcester is an attractive, small town of considerable antiquity. There is some evidence of neolithic settlement and of almost continuous Roman occupation in the first and second centuries. It was probably "the celebrated place called Alne", scene of the Ecclesiastical Council held in 709 by Ecgwin, Bishop of Worcester, to consecrate the Abbey of Evesham. The bishop seems to have had little success in the town however, for while preaching to the wealthy, hard-hearted people, his words were drowned by the hammering of the many smiths in the place. He therefore invoked divine retribution; the town was swallowed by an earthquake, and the site given to the Abbey of Evesham (Chronicle of Evesham, 24–27).

Despite the good bishop's curse, Alcester prospered, became a free borough in the reign of Henry I, sent two members to the parliament of 1275, and was granted a weekly market and an annual fair about the same time. Much woollen cloth was manufactured in the town, and a linen industry was established in Bleachfield Street in the 13th century. During the great coaching era in the early 19th century, Alcester gained new importance from being on the main route from London to Holyhead, with the Swan Hotel as the principal coaching inn.

(1) Henley Street was the site of the market from earliest times.

(2) The Market House, a two-storied building erected in 1618, was a gift to the town from Sir Fulke Greville, Lord of the Manor. Originally it was intended to be all in stone, but this must have proved too costly, and the upper storey was not completed in timber until 1641. The lower storey, originally an open stone colonnade where the covered market was held, was filled in in 1873. A plaque on the wall informs us that the building was bought from the Marquis of Hertford in 1919 to serve as a war memorial.

Butter Street, a short, narrow passage to the right of the Market House, is all that remains of the circle of shops and houses which once enclosed the churchyard, and was known as Shop Row. It still boasts a charming display of small bay windows, possibly the legacy of the shops.

Meeting House Lane, Alcester

(3) The rugged tower of St. Nicholas and its clock set obliquely to the High Street, are certainly eye-catching, but a closer inspection reveals that the church fabric is much restored, and the interior, though spacious, is rather nondescript, save for the highly coloured ceiling, which some may consider garish. Nonetheless, the dimensions of the building clearly indicate its importance, both as a religious house, and as a focal point for the town that grew round it. Conceivably because of the industries of linen and needle-making, non-conformity also thrived in Alcester. Evidence of this is to be found in Meeting Lane off Henley Street, where, just past a cottage whose door leans at a crazy angle, is a red-brick meeting house standing in an old graveyard, side by side with a Baptist chapel. On 3rd December 1688, a day which came to be known locally as "Running Thursday", a Protestant mob from the town demolished a private chapel which the Catholic Sir Robert Throckmorton had added to nearby Coughton Court.

(4) Malt Mill Lane has the oldest houses in the town; several dating from the early 16th century. Indeed one of the attractive features of Alcester is the ease with which buildings of all epochs and styles – Medieval, Tudor, Georgian, Regency, Victorian – rest cheek by jowl with one another, without any harsh clashes or tasteless intrusions on its architectural harmony. In Malt Mill Lane, at the entrance to Colebrook Close, a plaque on the wall tells us that the restoration of the surrounding timber-framed houses was begun in 1972 and completed in 1975 by Stratford-upon-Avon District Council, a most commendable piece of local government enterprise. The lane now looks much as it must have done centuries ago, apart perhaps from the roofs, and through the entry on the left is the most pleasant complex of old people's dwellings grouped round a green. We can walk through this and, from the end of Malt Mill Lane, enjoy the quiet prospect of the timber-framed houses at the top, whose oak beams are happily unmarred by artificial colouring.

(5) Bleachfield Street was the centre for needle-making, a cottage industry which survived here until quite recently. This is where Ryknield Street, which ran from the Fosse Way at Bourton-on-the-Water to Letocetum near Lichfield, connecting a series of minor settlements and forts, entered Alcester.

(6) Ragley Hall was built in 1680 from designs by Dr. Robert Hook, scientist and curator of the Royal Society, though its colonnades and porticos were the work of James Wyatt in 1780, and its gardens were laid out by Capability Brown at about the same time.

(7) Arrow Mill, now a fashionable restaurant, was mentioned in the Domesday Survey of 1086, and was still grinding corn a couple of decades ago. Hard by, amid buttercup-strewn meadows, is Arrow Church, burial place of the Seymours, Marquesses of Hertford, which with its old rectory forms a delightful corner of rural England.

(8) The church of St. Milburga at Wixford is kept locked, but the key is available at the nearby cottage. The church is notable, apart from its 12th century nave and 13th century chancel, for its south chapel, added in the 14th century by Thomas de Cruwe, Lord of the Manor. It contains the low altar tomb of grey marble upon which the probably life-sized brass effigies of Thomas and his wife Juliana, finished in fine detail, are to be found in all their glory. The man is in full plate armour of the period; his wife wearing a head-dress and veil, a close kirtle with buttoned sleeves and cuffs. Her mantle, open down the front, is held together with tasselled cords and rings. Sir Thomas was attorney to the Countess of Warwick, consort of the Kingmaker, which explains the

presence of the Warwick arms on the tomb, though mystery surrounds the intriguing, and oft-repeated representation of the human foot. The chapel also contains a 13th century chest of rough boarding, bound with heavy strap hinges of iron.

Immediately outside the church porch is an immense yew tree, whose outspread branches now require strong supports. In 1669, Wixford parishioners protested against the Rector's threats to have the ancient tree cut down, insisting "the like thereof is not to be found in all the diocese" ('Highways and Byways in Shakespeare's Country', W. Hutton, p 243). In 1730 the then Rector, Dr. Thomas, gave its height as 53 feet and its circumference as 18 feet 3 inches.

Shakespeare dubbed the village "Papist Wixford" because of the strong influence there of the Catholic Throckmortons of Coughton Court. The Wixford manor was in their possession from 1562 to 1919, and they maintained almshouses in the village as well as reserving the south chapel in the church for the saying of masses for the souls of Throckmortons departed.

(9) Shakespeare referred to "Dodging Exhall" because of the absence of any direct approach to it from Stratford, and indeed today it is still a quiet, pretty village well off the beaten track, in an area of fascinating historical associations, which is also well-suited to walkers.

WALK 14

BIDFORD-ON-AVON – MARLCLIFF – OFFENHAM – THE LITTLETONS – CLEEVE PRIOR – MARLCLIFF – BIDFORD-ON-AVON

Distances a.m. 4 miles, p.m. approximately 4½ miles.
O.S. Map No. 150 (Worcester and the Malverns), 1:50,000.
Start point, car park in Bidford recreation ground near Bidford bridge.
Grid reference 099517.

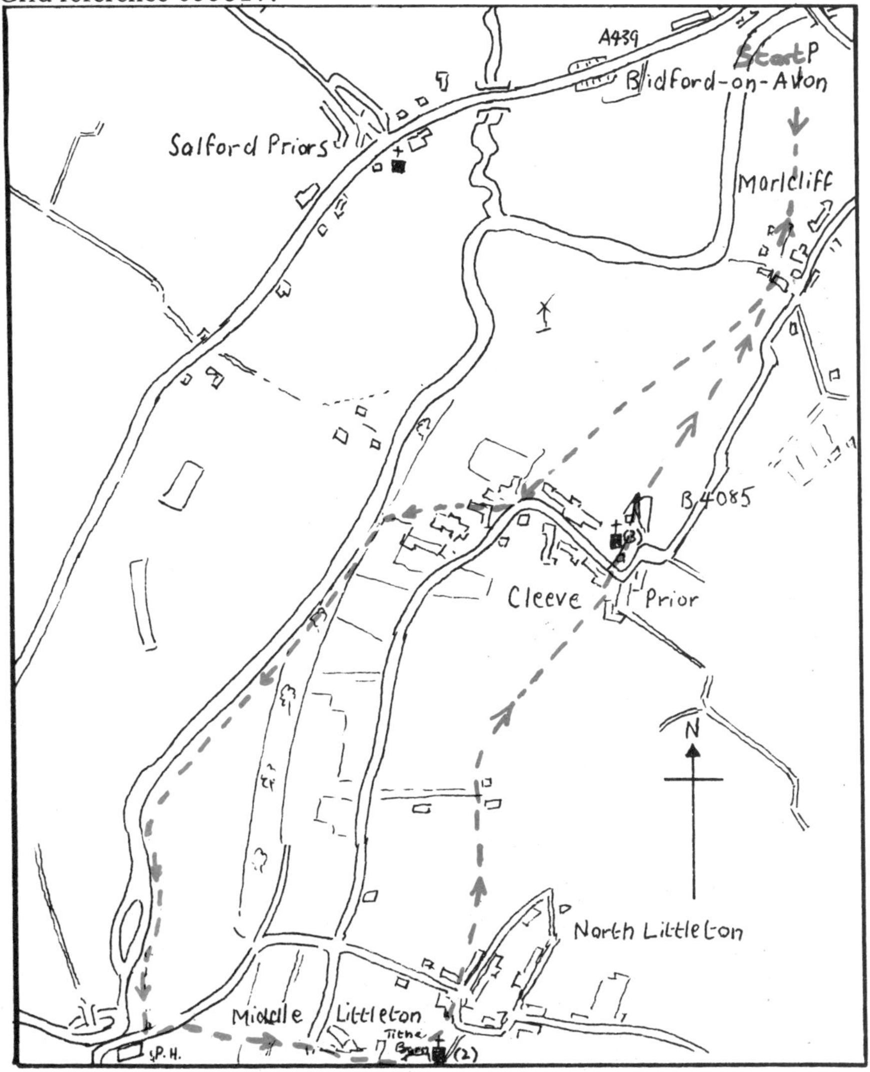

This is a longish walk, partly along the ridge of Cleeve Hill overlooking the smooth-flowing Avon, and partly among the market gardens of the Vale of Evesham (1) with its splendid churches, manors and tithe barns. The going is varied and easy, affording a panorama over the fertile fields, with brief forays into the viscous clinging clay of the Vale, which is notoriously heavy, but also infinitely rich.

15th Century Bridge, Bidford-on-Avon

Cross Bidford's ancient bridge and find the car park. From here the way goes left past the playing fields and behind the changing rooms. A gate ahead gives access to an arable field where the way keeps to the left to come upon a brook and a small pool. Tall willows overhang and the hedge is now on the right, with the barns and roofs of Marlcliff ahead over a stile and a pasture. There is an enclosed area with a narrow path on the right alongside a brook, and then some substantial cottages and a road. The road swings left, but our way goes straight on, winding uphill to the right across the red earth, eventually leading out on to the ridge. From here, there is a good view to the rear, over the smoking chimneys of Marlcliff, with Bidford in the hazy distance.

Soon the river comes into sight below, broad and slow-flowing over a weir, unhurried as it describes a huge, lazy oxbow. Carry on along the top of the ridge enjoying the air and the views. Just below, the ridge and furrow changes direction to run parallel to our path, betraying, perhaps , the former existence of an ancient settlement on this spot. Modern influence is apparent in the shape of a derelict wind pump ahead, and then Salford Priors can be seen across the river, with Cleeve Prior on the left, complemented by the copper spire of Harvington church on the right.

There is a gate in front, a stone house, and a road where young trees have been planted. Sadly, the maltreated hedgerows have been mauled almost to death. Then, past a brown, wooden building,the way goes down to a bridle way sign for Marlcliff to Mill Lane. Across this is the Cleeve Hill Nature Reserve, established by the Worcestershire Nature Conservation Trust, and opened by Lord Melchett in 1983. The track is now broad, flanked by trees and bushes which are a safe haven for birds, and just opposite a long drainage channel on the right bank of the river, a path descends to the water-meadows, which are thickly populated by sheep.

Go ahead through a lush pasture, long, with a rusting iron barn on the left, and a fishing hut opposite, to a stile. Various small fields and numerous stiles follow, all with notices absolutely forbidding the dipping of rod in the water, until a shaky footbridge leads past some houses to a wide weir, over which the river slides gently, and turns in a right-angle to the left. Harvington Mill stands here, forlorn and massive, and today herons haunt the spot. Now swing left along the verge and enter a huge caravan park, deserted in early spring, to emerge on to a road. A short stroll to the right and there is that well-known anglers' haven, the Fish and Anchor Inn. Clamorous at weekends, it has nevertheless good resources of food and drink.

Retrace steps up the road for about 150 yards, and opposite the entrance to the caravan park, turn right up a track lined with telephone posts. The way goes among cultivated lands to a cross-roads, then turns left uphill through the arable to a depression filled with scrub and bushes. This is an alternative route, for the footpath marked on the map is in danger of being ploughed out, save for faint traces among growing crops. The path leads from the road at about 45 degrees across the arable, then can be picked up as it ascends the hill through the coarse grass, and crosses the summit by a stile visible on the skyline. The track now affords easier going, winding gently upward, and giving views of the Cotswold Edge ahead, with Bredon Hill and the Malverns on the right, and the patchwork strips and glasshouses of Offenham in the middle distance. Over the top is a T-junction near some plum trees. Take the left-hand track past a concrete water storage dome, and continue to Middle Littleton past some huge plastic frames, and the corrugated sheds of a wholesale fruit and vegetable merchant, reaching the B4085 at some red-roofed cottages by a National Trust sign for the tithe barn.

Either cross directly over the road and go down School Lane, or go left for about 100 yards, and take the footpath signposted North Littleton, which keeps the objectives – the barn and the church – in sight. It crosses two rickety stiles and goes by the back of some houses to a red metal gate on the right, whence it passes via a path on the left, to the towering buttressed entrance, and steep-pitched tiled roof of the massive building (2).

Retrace steps and turn left for the church where, in the right hand corner of the churchyard is a path, skirting a garden with a stile at the end leading into a meadow. Carry on and come soon to a ploughed field, where deviate left, then right along the border to come to a road. Here are enormous clumps of rhubarb, testimony to the soil's wealth, and the skill of those who manage it. Cross the road at a signpost to Cleeve Prior, and walk along the side of a wide field of strip cultivation, passing more triffid-like rhubarb, patches of sage, sprouts and leeks, and an enclosure of more Jacob sheep with their black offspring. This medieval landscape continues, and where the track divides near some willows, go straight on over a footbridge and towards the beckoning tower of Cleeve Prior church (3).

The track leads on to a little village green, where stands the mouldering hulk of an ancient tree, long held in the strangling grip of clinging ivy; a calm, lovely spot, the one–time village centre, complete with mounting block and cottages grouped round the church. Go through the churchyard towards a line of poplars and a yellow marker. On the right is an old manor house, and behind it another barn. The way goes over a footbridge and through three sheep pastures, then an arable field, where it follows the hedge on the right, before swinging left up to a hedge gap. Through this and across the orchard beyond is a stile marking the County boundary with Warwickshire. The yellow markers now desert the track, but there are two more meadows and stiles before the ground descends to the red marl country again, where, by a thatched cottage with a modern extension, the route taken at the start of the ramble leads back to Bidford.

(1) Market gardening and fruit growing have been practised in the Vale of Evesham since the 18th century, but the coming of the railways in the 19th century allowed the easy transportation of the produce to the markets of Birmingham whilst it was still in prime condition, and caused a huge expansion in the industry. After the agricultural depression of the 1870s, individual growers of small means were able to buy up strips of land and work them successfully, producing fruit and vegetable crops for which there was a demand. Sometimes these strips were in different districts and with diverse soil conditions, which enabled growers to produce quite different, and often specialist crops such as asparagus, as well as the familiar fruit and vegetables, for which there was always a ready demand.

This strip system of small-holdings is clearly visible from any elevated point, and forms a marked contrast to the dreary monoculture of ordinary arable farming. Early Dutch influence in horticulture is evident on all sides, in the extensive use of glasshouses which are a prominent feature of the Vale. The so-called Evesham custom whereby every gardener can tend and develop his land as he wishes, and grow crops of his own choosing, retaining a say in the nomination of his successor from whom he can claim compensation for improvements made, is now giving way to the more intensive methods of the big operators. Indeed, the whole industry now has to compete with the Common Market on terms which are by no means as favourable as for normal farming, but still around Offenham in particular, the mark of the small-holder's spade can be seen in the multitude of strips of differing crops. From the ridge of Cleeve Hill, the varying colours and alignments of the plots in the large open fields, recalls the appearance of the medieval landscape, and this impression is reinforced by the presence of ridge and furrow, where the small holder has seen fit not to dig.

The interest of this area is enhanced by the River Avon, which meanders through it and in its long history has formed various terraces or changes of level. The river's flood plain must once have covered a vast area of the flat lands, where it deposited the alluvial soils which are its fertile legacy. Sometimes erosion has left earlier terraces exposed, and these have formed river cliffs such as Cleeve Hill, where the red marls have been brought to the surface, and now contrast colourfully with the yelllowish clay of the Vale. Cleeve Hill is quite precipitous and runs from Marlcliff to Bennetts Hill Farm, and without doubt the river is slowly eroding its foot. Further evidence of this imperceptible movement in the river bed is to be found in the many weirs, not all man-made, and in the many rises and falls in the river's level, some of which have been exploited by man to use as fords, heads of water and mill races. The region has a flavour and character all its own, and stands in sharp contrast to the region of the upper Avon valley.

Medieval Tithe Barn, Middle Littleton

(2) The medieval tithe barn at Middle Littleton is still in use, and is most impressive with its wagon bays and slit windows, suggesting a former economic power base of prime importance. Whether it was the "very fine grange at Littleton" attributed to Abbot John of Brokehampton, 1282 – 1379, its distinct esslesiastical appearance is a striking token of the power and wealth of the Abbey of Evesham to which it belonged. Indeed it must rival its more famous fellow at Bredon for size and grandeur. In its cavernous interior are to be seen the great crucks reinforced by massive arched struts, which support the weight of the stone tiles. On the floor, the huge flag stones formed a secure base for the loaded wagons bringing their tributes of produce for the Abbey.

(3) The beautiful church at Cleeve Prior has an admirable 13th century tower, with battlements and assorted gargoyles, but the very peace of the place belies all evil influence. The 13th century nave has outward bulging walls and twisted roof beams. The font and worked pew ends are probably 14th century, as is the chancel and its piscina in the south wall. Beneath the bell ropes is a huge elm chest, hewn from a single tree trunk, and of similar age to the pew ends. For centuries the Prior and Chapter of Worcester Cathedral were lords of the manor, and clearly gave the parish its name.

WALK 15

SHURNOCK COURT – FECKENHAM – MORTON UNDERHILL – SHURNOCK COURT

Distances, a.m. 4 miles, p.m. approximately 4½ miles.
O.S. Map No. 150 (Worcester and the Malverns), 1:50,000.
Start point lay-by on B4090, opposite Shurnock Court. Grid reference 027609.

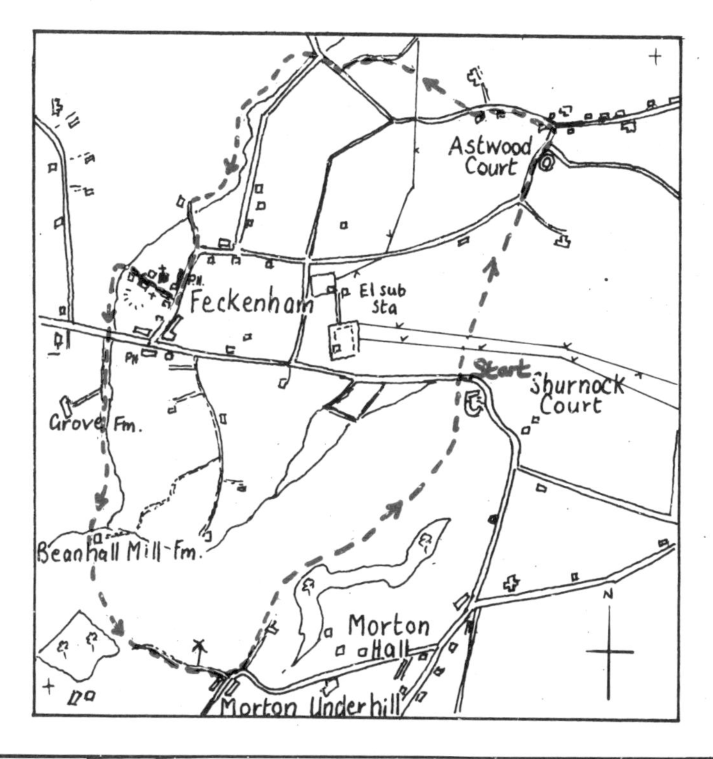

This walk, in the area once covered by the vast Feckenham forest, starts with a short, sharp climb, and then levels out to pass through quiet pastures, along shady lanes, and by cool streams. We are reminded of the ancient forest by the presence of tall oaks; and the abundance of fine houses, many with moats, bears witness to the former prosperity of the district.

Park in the lay-by and go down the road a few yards for a glimpse of the magnificent Elizabethan hall-house, a symphony in black and white. What better way to secure peace and privacy than by surrounding

Shurnock Court

a house with water? At the lay-by, find a finger-post indicating Mutton Hall. It stands amid a pile of rubbish near a blue and white sign, vainly asking for litter to be taken home. The path is diverted slightly to the left and passes through a metal gate in a tall hedge. There follows a climb to a dominant mound surmounted by two pylons. At the top, pass through another metal gate and look back on the view, before walking along the ridge path under two minor power lines, keeping the second pylon on the left. Descend the stony track to a gate in the end of the field. Here is a road with a finger-post for Shurnock. Go right and pass some delapidated farm buildings, then the moated Astwood Court, and a side road to Astwood Bank. Turn left at the next junction along the lane for Ham Green and Elcocks brook, keeping a square red-brick Victorian house on the right.

The shady lane passes beneath tall ashes and oaks. A large modern house on the left has a swimming pool and stables. Leave the sign-post to Crabbs Cross and the entry to Astwood Hill farm on the right, and look for two holly trees standing in the hedge on that side. A gate between them admits to a pasture. Follow the wire fence on the right until level with a pylon, then turn about 20 degrees left and descend below some cables to a stile and a footbridge in the facing hedge. Go up the sloping meadow to a stile with a Country Landowner's waymarker on the reverse side. Turn left past the imposing property of Old Yarr and its lake. Once again there are plenty of trees, with willows lining the stream. Go right at the T-junction and right again over a bridge, then pass through the gate immediately on the left. Now follow Bow Brook over several meadows for about a mile to Dunstall Court on the right, climbing stiles and using hedge gaps.

At Dunstall find a footbridge on the left under a chestnut tree, and cross the brook. In front are two stiles with a concrete culvert between. Cross the next field to the right-hand corner where there is a stile by a white gate, and the road. On the right a footpath runs alongside the road to the churchyard. Take it, leave the churchyard by the main gate, cross the green and the Rose and Crown opposite offers very good fare.

Refreshed, go through the churchyard, keeping to the left of the tower, and find a path to the cricket field. Just behind the pavilion is a track going right. Pass the entry to Old Mill House, and go through the gate posts, following the path which leaves the mill pool on the right, crosses the stream by a foot-bridge and bears left alongside it under the trees. It rises to a junction of paths, goes left by a hedge, then descends to the stream and continues to the road by White Brook House.

Opposite is a marked bridle-way to Morton Underhill. The lane passes a wind pump on the right and goes on to a bend where there are two facing gates. Go through the one on the right, across the pasture, and under the ash trees with the hedge on the right, to another metal gate. Go through this to follow the hedge on the right round the field to a gate in the right-hand corner. Continue to a stream and hedge ahead; go right for about 60 yards, then turn left over a foot-bridge. Follow the indicated way up the meadow with the tall hedge on the left, to a gate. Sloes and hawthorn prevail here, with occasional crab apples. Keep going ahead through two more metal gates, following the telephone wires, and when these diverge, look for a red metal gate on the left. Through this a rough track leads by another wind pump to the hamlet of Morton Underhill. Turn left down the lane, which soon dips left again and leads to a farm.

Go through the farm buildings to the left of the house to a blue gate into a field. Across it is another blue gate and a notice asking walkers to "use the headland please". Do so, by going right and walking between the power-lines and the oaks fringing the base of the overhanging ridge. There are field maples and fox earths here. A metal hunting-gate slightly to the left admits to the next field, with a similar request to use the headland. Continue along the border on the right and look for a metal gate by an oak, half left in the facing hedge. The next field is long, with pronounced ridge and furrow. It has a gate in the left corner, again close by an oak.

Follow the wire fence on the right past a water trough and a line of oaks on the left, to another gate. Turn right along the bridle path under power lines towards the ridge, and after 100 yards, there is a gap and a gate on the left. Cross the ridge and furrow towards the splendid old house, making for the twin pylons on the hill behind. On the right is a long mound, probably the spoil from the moat, and from here there is a good view of the gabled end of the house behind its protecting water. Cross the foot-bridge ahead, below the willows, and aim for a gate in the right-hand corner of the field. This gate leads on to the B4090 – the Roman Salt Way from Droitwich – with the lay-by just across it.

Feckenham today is a pleasant village partly straggling along the B4090 – that long, straight road from Droitwich to Alcester, both places important to the Romans. Salt has always been a commodity vital to man; hence the early development of Droitwich as a salt-pan, with distributive roads radiating from it. Feckenham was on one of the salt routes leading west through the great forest which at its greatest extent stretched from Worcester to the Warwickshire border. Feckenham was roughly in the centre, and as the largest of the villages dotted among the forest clearings, it became the natural administrative centre for the whole area.

As the great woodland increased in size, the other villages became increasingly isolated and depopulated, while Feckenham grew, attracting displaced people, and exercising complete local jurisdiction throughout the early Middle Ages. The stringent forest laws, forbidding the hunting of game, grazing of pigs and cattle, and ordering the de-clawing of all dogs were rigidly enforced by the forest wardens, and Feckenham's now vanished prison must often have been crowded with unfortunate poachers and other offenders against the royal writ.

Later the village prospered from the sale of timber for the developing iron industries, but the biggest source of deforestation must have been the incessant demand for wood for use in salt-boiling at Droitwich. This was to be the primary cause of the almost complete disappearance of the great forest, for there was then no regular policy of replanting. Thus, with the passing of the mighty trees with which it was once surrounded, Feckenham itself passed into comparative obscurity, though it still possesses some handsome houses to remind us of its former grandeur.

The church, though much restored, is by no means to be slighted. The squat, rugged tower presides over a long nave where there are three solid tables of the local black oak, beneath the painted arches. Sir Martyn Culpeper of nearby Astwood Court (modernised but still moated), has a memorial tablet in the chancel. A pair of wooden wafer tongs used in the baking of sacred wafers was discovered near the home of Feckenham's most famous son, John de Feckenham, whose image still gazes down benignly from one of the chancel windows. He was educated by the monks of Evesham Abbey, and remained a staunch Catholic throughout his life, suffering long terms of imprisonment under both Henry VIII and Elizabeth for his religious convictions. For a brief period in the reign of Mary Tudor he reaped the reward for his constancy, for she made him the last Abbot of Westminster, and charged him with the reconversion of former Catholics. It seems that he was entirely free of bigotry, and cruelty was not in his nature, so that he was often moved to intercede with his zealous mistress on behalf of those who could never recounce their new faith, and was instrumental in saving the lives of many.

John de Feckenham died after long years of honourable imprisonment in the reign of Elizabeth who respected him always, and released him to minister to the poor during the last months of his life. When he died in 1585, his charitable principles and generosity of spirit, served as an example to all in an age of bitter religious prejudice and intolerance.

WALK 16

BLAKEDOWN–HARVINGTON HALL–HILLPOOL–BLAKEDOWN

Distance, a.m. 3 miles, p.m. approximately 4 miles.
O.S. Map No. 139 (Birmingham), 1:50,000.
Start point Blakedown station approach. Grid reference 881787.

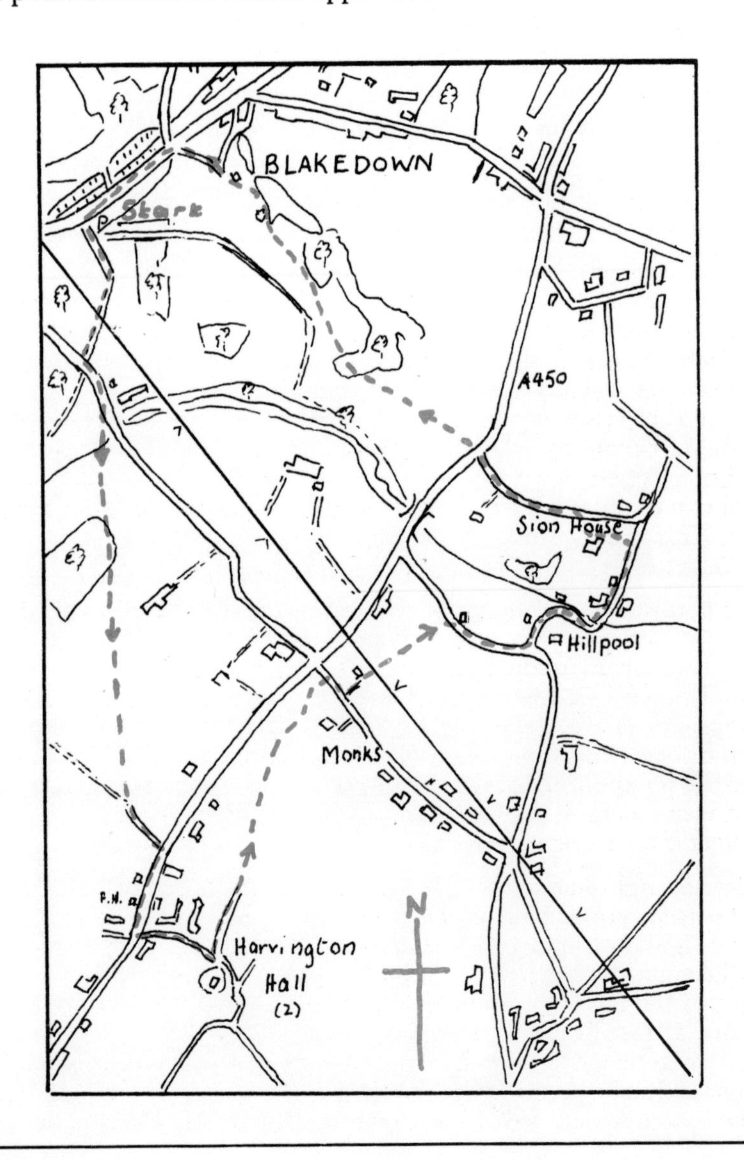

This walk is flat, through sandy farmland and along lanes in some of the most delightful countryside of North Worcestershire. It also takes the rambler near to two of the most interesting buildings in this part of England, viz: the fine medieval church of Chaddesley Corbett (1), and the evocative, intriguing Harvington Hall (2). Both are monuments to the power of the Christian faith and to man's determination to practise that faith in the way he thinks best.

Blakedown is a long, straggling township astride the bustling A456, and the church and the railway station are useful points of reference. Park in Station Approach and turn right down the busy main street to a long railway viaduct on the right. Opposite the last archway is a lane which can be an alternative parking place. Halfshire Lane goes off to the right, but the one opposite soon gives on to a footpath half-right at a junction, near some houses and rhododendron bushes. The path narrows and wends its way uphill beneath the trees, and then opens out by a white house with some Scots pines standing on the left.

At a junction turn right along a metalled road, past bungalows and houses, beneath oaks and past a large white house, 'Blakedown Rough', on the left. There is a waymarked bridleway leading off to the left, which becomes a sandy track, lined with shrubs and pines, but this too opens out as it passes an open, grassy field and banks of bracken. It turns sharp right, becoming even more sandy, and descends beneath power lines through open fields towards a wood and a group of buildings. The path joins a farm road which comes in at right-angles, and swings left along it. This is easy walking in flat country, but the sand could be very sticky in wet weather.

Just before a farm on the left, take a waymarked bridleway through a metal gate on the right. The way now goes half-left past a heap of manure, through an arable field, by two isolated oaks, under more power lines, and down to a line of trees and a brook ahead. Across the brook pass another oak on the right, walk through ankle-deep sand over another bridge and along a woodland track lined with willow herb and bracken. After the hot trudge through the fields, the shade is refreshing, and the way emerges from the wood into a sandy dell near a silver birch tree. There is a parting of the ways here.

Take the right-hand track, leaving a domed hill on the left. The path winds up past more silver birches to a small plateau, giving good views. Take the right fork alongside an arable field and then skirt the soft-fruit bushes keeping the hedge on the right. Follow the well-used way around the right of the second currant field and carry on to the road. Turn right and arrive at the Talbot or Dog Inn, for it seems to be known by both names. There is soft, clear ale here with good food, and time to enjoy both before Harvington Hall opens at 2 o'clock. Leave the Dog Inn and take the road opposite past a Council estate and a long-disused quarry on the right, which once supplied stone for the Hall. Then there are stew-ponds, a farm, a church, and finally the old manor house, seeming to float dreamily on its moat, sheltered by overhanging trees.

Should a visit to the Hall not be desired, return to the quarry opposite which is a track skirting an arable field beyond an ash tree. In the top right–hand corner is a plum orchard. Cross into it, and keeping the plum trees on the left, leave the orchard and walk along the right-hand edge of a long root vegetable field, with the A450 not far off to the left. A stile is in the top right-hand corner, and gives access to a pasture bordered by a tall hazel hedge. Turn left in the top right-hand corner and follow the hedge down to a stile on the right which may require a little finding, but is there nonetheless. A herd of Highland cattle graze in the field on the right, so do not stray, but keep straight ahead towards an imposing white house called 'Monks', and come soon to a road with a waymark sign pointing in the direction you have come. Climb the stile on to the road, turn right, and almost at once left on to a track under some high tension wires, to a white gate in a field. In the left-hand corner is another gate, and the way lies through this, and half-right across a pasture in the direction of a white house. At the field boundary is a stile with a rather long drop into a lane.

Turn right now to ascend the lane, swinging left past Grafton Cottage, with its distinctive leaded windows, on the corner. The quiet lane climbs steadily to give some pleasing views, and is lined with elder flowers in profusion. On the banksides the foxgloves nod gently in the breeze. The fields are scented with sweet hay. Presently the white facade of Sion House comes into sight on the hill to the left. Turn left at a junction to descend into Hillpool with its quarry, its quiet dwellings and busy little brook. The lane now rises steeply amid vetches, ash trees and more foxgloves, till there is a glimpse at the summit, of a tall steeple on the right, and the Clent Hills ahead in the distance. Here, leave the lane turning left along a bridle way through Sion Farm buildings, then left again past the dozing farm kittens, and right at a red arrow pointing the route up past some green-painted sheds. Now it is straight ahead, down a pleasant track passing Sion House lodge on the left, where live some noisy but affable labradors, and so on to the A450. Cross the road and walk up a steep little path, go through an iron gate and walk along an elevated plateau giving commanding views on both sides. After about half a mile, make a slow descent amid the bushes to a metalled track with Blakedown now in sight. Turn right down the track, and continue along it, ignoring the first bridle path sign on a corner. Instead look for another sign further on leading to Ladies' Pool, a local fishing lake. Skirt the pool and find a choice of two paths back to the town. A nice walk, with fair physical activity balanced by aesthetic pleasures.

(1) In Chaddesley Corbett's long and ancient street, 17th century half-timbered houses blend comfortably with their Georgian neighbours.. The place was important and wealthy in the Middle Ages, as is amply proved by the spacious nave of St. Cassian's church. Here is the history of the village write large in stone, dating from the first foundations in the 12th century. The unusual dedication is of mysterious origin, but to the imaginative, the most appealing story is that Cassian was a Christian schoolmaster done to death with iron stili by his pagan pupils. This unhappy event presumably took place during the Roman persecution of the Christians, and was not a normal breach of school discipline. In the churchyard stands an old schoolhouse dating from 1809, probably built on the site of an earlier one, and the present school is also nearby.

The church founded by Richard Folliott, the Norman lord of the manor in the 12th century, consisted of a nave, chancel and north aisle, but already by the 13th century, the church had proved too small for the growing community, and the new lords, the Corbetts, added a south aisle. The tower and spire were added in the 14th century, and when the Corbett family died out, the parish passed into the possession of St. Mary's church, Warwick, in 1394. One of the most striking of the early features is the 12th century font, so unmistakably Norman with its plaited stone band round the top, intended to ward off evil spirits. The east window is very rich and impressive for a parish church, as is the chancel with its piscina and canopied sedilia and aumbry. The recessed tomb in the south wall, also canopied, was probably intended for the last of the Corbetts. Though extensive restoration has impaired the original appeareance of the interior, one still has an overwhelming feeling of space which the presence of the pews does not destroy as it so often does in parish churches.

Catholic influence was strong in the area and in 1772, Sir Robert Throckmorton, now the lord of the manor, commissioned an architect to view the tower and spire, which was rebuilt by James Rose and James Haywood, both Chaddesley men. The money was raised with the aid of eight levies on the local inhabitants, and the finished work can be justly compared with that of nearby Bromsgrove. Further renovations were carried out in the 19th century, making a rich inheritance which comprises the stone effigies of the Corbetts, the brasses of Thomas and Margaret Forest (he was the 'parker' of Dunclent Park), and a wealth of delicately carved masonry.

(2) Harvington Hall retains an aura of mystery, of inaccessibility, of lurking danger perhaps. This was where the Catholics worshipped in secret all those years ago, furtively watching through the mullioned win-

dows, and fearfully expecting the clattering approach of their persecutors across the drawbridge and the loud alarums at the gate.

Now the old house is peaceful and undistrubed, its Turod brick superstructure resting solidly on its sandstone base, its tall chimneys pointing towards the heaven so ardently desired by its former inmates. Inside, all is dim and cool, and unchanged throughout the centuries. There is a priest-hole above the oven and under the garde-robe, another behind a false beam in Dr. Dodd's library. Dr. Dodd was in fact an alias for Dr. Toothill, the chaplain of the Hall.

Lady Yate's nursery is next to a chapel decorated with tear drops representing the blood and tears of Christ, the chapel windows look out over the moat to give early warning of the raiders' approach, and enabling the priest to take refuge in his bolt hole, not one of which was ever discovered at Harvington. The whole household assembled once a day for mass in the chapel, whose altar fittings were only displayed for the services, and could be speedily concealed in a shallow recess under the floorboards in the event of a sudden interruption.

In the staircase brought from Coughton Court, another Catholic stronghold, is a further priest-hole skilfully hidden beneath a tread. In fact the whole place is still redolent of those troubled times, reminding us that purges and persecutions, whether religious or political, are no new phenomena, nor limited to our own age.

WALK 17

BEWDLEY – RIBBESFORD – BEWDLEY

Distances 2½ or 4½ miles.
O.S. Map No. 138 (Kidderminster and Wyre Forest), 1:50,000.
Car park and start point in Dog Lane, just beyond St. Anne's church.
Grid reference 786753.

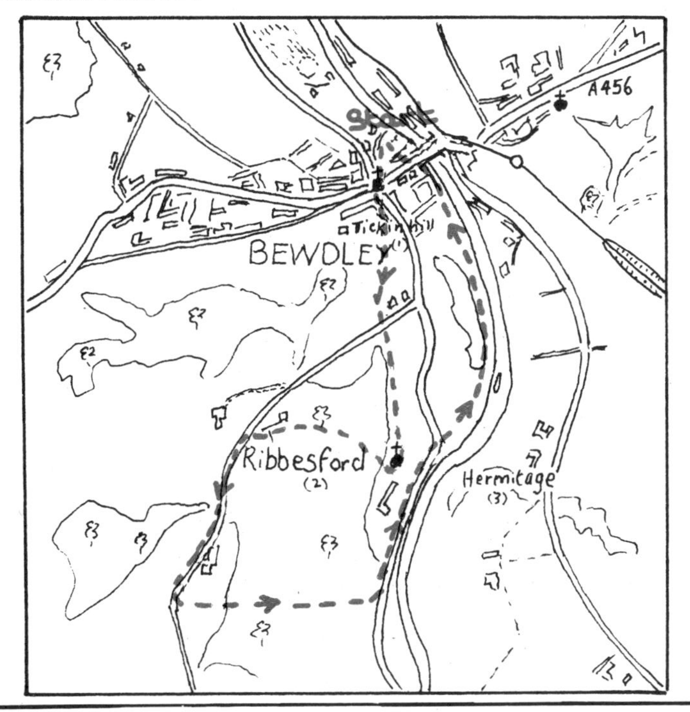

In spite of its proximity to industrial Kidderminster, Bewdley has retained its own unique identity, and should be explored on foot, at leisure, before the easy, level ramble to Ribbesford is started. The route goes over meadow and alongside ploughed land to the church at Ribbesford, and returns by a riverside path which can be muddy and slippery in wet weather, but there are no hills to climb or awkward ground to cover. It is hoped that the notes on Bewdley will enable the enquiring walker to enjoy a morning visit, followed by a bar lunch at the George Hotel or perhaps the Redthorpe Hotel in High Street, before embarking on one of the suggested routes.

From Dog Lane go past the Horn and Trumpet inn, turn left past the church, then right up Park Lane for about 100 yards. Take the footpath on the left behind the almshouses and walk along the brick path to a kissing gate. The way then goes alongside a corrugated fence on the left, and the elevated site of Tickenhill Manor (1), is on the right. Go through another gate past some chestnut fencing, leaving a large pond on the right as the path descends. Some large oaks flank the route on the left before it rises under lime trees, to come to a road, across which the way leads on the left of an arable field, down to a rough track. The church of St. Leonard's is on the right at the bottom of the track, and opposite a group of large barns.

For the short route, turn left down a lane lined with horse chestnut trees to the B4194. Ribbesford House (2) with its twin cupolas, is on the right. Turn left along the road to the corner where it goes sharp left, and find a gap on the right leading to the river bank. Walk to the left through clumps of comfrey and balsam giving glimpses of the river, wide and smooth, on the right. It is now easy and pleasant going, and soon Blackstone Rock (3) appears on the opposite bank, then the sports ground on the left comes into sight, and the quayside and bridge immediately after.

For the longer route, take the stepped path from the churchyard and go over a stile, up alongside the hedge and into the wood. Cross the stile and then the next one near a gate. Go straight along the farm track and then left along the road to Glebe Cottage, where the way goes slightly left of the cottage and passes through a gateway. Go left again and across the main track downhill to a Y-junction, where go right and then fork right again to go down the path to the Woodman Inn. Now go left along the road to the point where it turns sharp left, and find the entry to the river bank as for the short walk.

Bewdley, today an attractive, elegant Georgian town, graced by a superb Thomas Telford bridge, was originally Wribbenhall in Saxon times, and was renamed Beau Lieu when the manor and estate were given by the Conqueror to Roger de Mortimer, the powerful Marcher baron whose task was to keep the peace along the Welsh border. The Mortimers came to rule most of the Welsh border lands based on Wigmore and Ludlow castles, and a Welsh Gate still stood in Bewdley until 1822.

John Leland visited the town in 1540 and described it as "set on the syd of an hill so coningly that a man cannot wishe to set a towne better. It riseth from the Severne banke so that a man standing on the hill trans pontem by este may descrive every house in the towne, and at the rysinge of the sonne the whole towne gliterithe, being all of new buyldinge, as it were of gold" (Itinerary: 1535–1543).

Charles I visited Bewdley several times, the last being on the 17th June 1645, following the Royalist defeat at Naseby. The Parliamentary troops had so damaged Tickenhill Manor that the King was forced to spend the night at the Angel Inn.

From earliest times there were industries here – tanneries, cap-making, and the fashioning of household articles from horn, but the quays on either bank of the river are reminders of the most prosperous days of Bewdley in the 18th century, as a busy inland port and trading centre. Because at that era the roads were often seas of mud in the winter,or deserts of dust in the summer, permitting at best only the passage of lightly loaded pack-horses, or cumbrous, slow-moving carts, the rivers were widely used as the main arteries of transport. Bristol was the main port of the south-west, and from it the Severn penetrated right into the interior of the country, carrying more traffic than any other river, and much of it destined for onward distribution from Bewdley, the furthest navigable point.

Upstream came wine, spices, tea, sugar, cotton and even slaves, if the Black Boy Inn does not belie its name. The river ports of the Midlands in return shipped out the local products of cloth, wool, timber, cheese, and later metal, keeping their quaysides constantly busy, and bringing wealth to their merchants. At Bewdley, the merchants used some of this wealth to build their handsome Georgian houses on the river banks or in Load Street. The fine, classically-simple St. Anne's church was built at the same time to replace the ancient wooden structure. Its graceful, uncluttered interior has Venetian windows and Doric columns, with the town's coat-of-arms – an anchor over a rose and a sword enclosed in a fetterlock – prominently displayed above the motto: 'Pro Deo, Rege, Grege' – 'For God, the King, and the People'.

As navigation became more difficult north of the bridge, the cargoes were unloaded on the quays and transferred to smaller, flat-bottomed boats called trowes, which were built in the town, and these were dragged upstream by labourers known as bow-hauliers, who were clearly a rough, lawless breed. When in 1761 Parliament passed an Act which permitted horses to be used to pull river boats, it met with the most violent opposition from the bow-hauliers, whose headquarters were the Mug House on Coles Quay, where traditionally they met, were hired to haul boats, and sealed their contracts with a mug of ale.

In the 1760s it was proposed that James Brindley should be engaged to plan and build a canal linking the Severn and the Trent–Mersey canal near Bewdley. Stubbornly, the proud corporation refused to have anything to do with "the stinking ditch", and as a result Brindley constructed the Staffordshire–Worcestershire canal to enter the Severn at Lower Mitton, which rapidly developed into the inland port of Stourport, and Bewdley's trade dwindled correspondingly.

Now the Museum on the site of the old Shambles in Load Street reflects aspects of the town's former prosperity – local crafts, such as rope-making, smithing, brass-founding and coopering are displayed in arcades along a cobbled street, at the end of which are two tiny cells for the detention of malefactors. There is also a brass foundry which turns out artefacts on a commercial basis, and a show-case containing mementoes of the town's most famous son, Stanley Baldwin, who was Prime Minister in the '20s and '30s. Across the river is the busy working station of the Severn Valley Steam Railway.

(1) Tickenhill, the Manor built by the Mortimers west of the town, was enlarged by Richard, Duke of York, who also provided the town with its first bridge in 1447. His son, Edward, Earl of March, the future Edward IV, lived for a time at Tickenhill, and granted the town a charter in 1472 in return for the support of Bewdley men at the Battle of Tewkesbury, where he finally destroyed the forces of Queen Margaret, and brought an end to the Wars of the Roses.

In 1499, Prince Arthur, the eldest son of Henry VII, was betrothed by proxy to Catherine of Aragon, at Tickenhill Manor. Shortly after his marriage to the Spanish princess, he died of pneumonia at Ludlow Castle, and on 25th April 1502 his body rested at Tickenhill on its way to Worcester Cathedral. This tragic affair was to be fraught with dire consequences, for his brother Henry VIII later married Catherine, and the course of English history was changed as a result.

(2) Ribbesford House south of the town was once the home of the powerful Beauchamp family, and later that of the 17th century poet George Herbert. In World War II it was for a time the training centre for the officers of the Free French Forces. The little church of St. Leonard is interesting for its Norman tympanum, depicting a knight transfixing a monster with his bow and arrow. The building was struck by lightning and had to be partially rebuilt in 1877 with columns of wood and stone. At the west end is a pleasant window by William Morris after a design by Burne-Jones.

(3) The caves on the east side of the river below the town at Blackstone Rock, were used as a hermitage in the Middle Ages, and also provided shelter for travellers who were held up when the river was too high to ford, before the building of the 15th century bridge. Until the middle of the 19th century, the Severn was tidal to this point, and vessels commonly moored here to await the tidal bore to carry them up to the quays at Bewdley.

Beau Lieu, Coles Quay, Load Street – evocative words indeed, which sum up to perfection this historic and delightful Severnside town.

WALK 18

KINGSFORD COUNTRY PARK – KINVER EDGE – KINVER VILLAGE – KINGSFORD COUNTRY PARK

Distances a.m. 3½ miles, p.m. 3 miles.
O.S. Map No. 138 (Kidderminster and Wyre Forest), 1:50,000.
Start point Car Park in the Country Park. Grid ref. 825823.

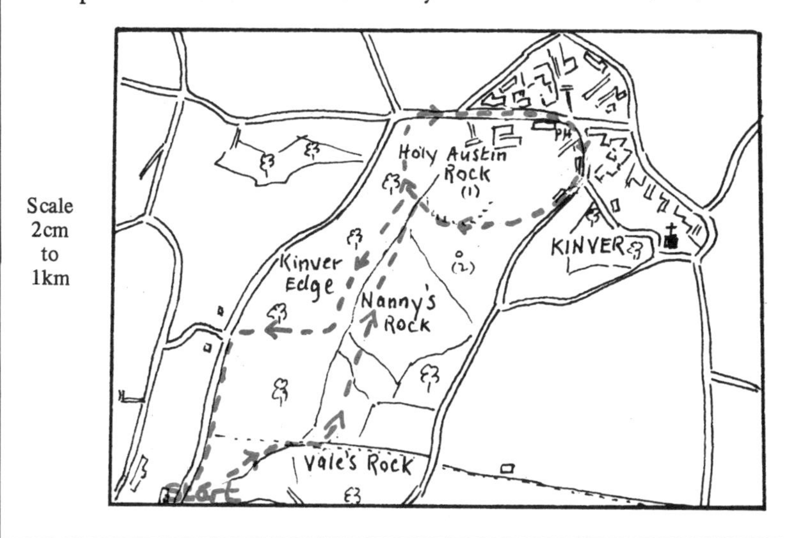

The walk entails a climb by sandy paths, amid woods, from 70 to 164 metres, a descent to Kinver, and a steady climb back to the Edge after lunch. The rewards for this moderate effort are extensive views from the summit, and clean fresh air. The car park, furnished with toilets and display maps of the area, is actually in Hereford and Worcester, but diagonally left from the information board is a sign pointing the way up to Kinver Edge, with the Staffordshire Knot on it.

A sandy trail leads up between bracken and birch. The latter are shallow-rooted and spindly, but presently at a massive oak, the way goes right and more stiffly uphill. Soon, outcrops of red sandstone appear, and occasional, large erratic rocks stand out among the trees. Rowan and foxglove like this terrain, and further ascent brings into sight a blue marker, then a glade with a sign-post to Mow Cop, 83 metres. The Staffordshire Way now goes left up to the Cop, from which there are the first views east and west. Soon on the left is a short diversion to Vista Seat, and a prospect of distant Brown Clee opens up over the top of a sea of birch trees. Further on are more seats amid patchwork scrub oak, magnificent views over Wenlock Edge, and in the valley on the right a glimpse of Enville Hall and church.

From the iron-age fort on the summit, extensive and flat, with sheer drops, Birmingham's high-rise towers are clearly visible, while Kinver village sprawls at our feet, with the Lickey Hills away in the distance, on the right. This is a favourite spot for bladder campion and mallow, growing among the piles of brushwood placed around the edges of the escarpment to prevent the unwary from venturing too close to the edge. A curving path goes off down to the left (or right if you are retracing your steps from the end of the ridge), which soon reaches a steep sandstone outcrop, once a wide, water cascade. A rocky descent on the left of this is flanked by clumps of bilberries, and leads down to a grassy open space, with a large rock near a road.

A diversion up a stairway brings the walker to the fantastic outcrop know as Holy Austin Rock (1), with its troglodite dwellings, then a return to the road will bring him quickly to Kinver village. Turn right, and the Plough and Harrow will offer good food, most cheerfully served, with palatable locally-brewed ale.

Kinver has a wide main street with pleasant buildings and a red sandstone church perched on a commanding height, but the afternoon walk does not lie that way, but goes left out of the inn and left again up the street and past the school. This area is known as the Compa. At a T-junction go left, and after about a hundred yards, at a de-restriction sign, go up a made-up path to the right, among the houses. This leads into open heath and goes straight up the facing slope to the top of the Edge. On the left across a broad, open space, is a plaque (2) set in a boulder and alongside a memorial obelisk. Straight ahead a path by a tall hedge, leads past a group of conifers and a large shelter. Take it. The way now becomes sandy underfoot and goes alongside a wire fence, with fields on the left. The Malverns and Bredon Hill are now visible on a clear day. Keep going for about a mile until you enter an oak glade and come to a junction of tracks. Go left and continue down the same track as in the morning to come once more to Mow Cop. Descend to the right, go left at a blue marker, and continue down by a network of tracks to the road and the car park.

Kingsford Park, 200 acres of fine heath and woodland, was given to Kidderminster by John Britton, a carpet manufacturer, and adjoins another 200 acres of National Trust property which includes Kinver Edge. The name 'Kinver' has several possible derivations, among them 'Cynibre', a great hill, or as in the Domesday Survey, 'Chenavare'. All of course refer to the great ridge in what was once a vast Mercian forest. The area was settled at a much earlier period, by the evidence of the large iron-age fort, now covered by gorse, broom and birch. Like Cannock Chase, it was a hunting place for early kings, and again like Cannock Chase, it is now an extensive playground for the people of the nearby conurbations. The massive rocks of red, friable sandstone on the north face of the hill are a veritable warren of caves and hollows which have been burrowed out of the soft rock. They are probably part of the iron-age settlement, but were still inhabited less than 30 years ago, and represent the last genuine troglodite dwellings in England.

(1) One of the rocks, known as Holy Austin Rock, was populated throughout the Middle Ages by hermits, whilst another called Nanny's Rock has elaborate windows and chimneys carved into it. Both have served as human habitations, and Holy Austin Rock was certainly occupied until about 1955. The soft stone is easily worked, enabling the cave-dwellers to enlarge their accommodation without excessive labour. Nor were they under undue hardship, for they had clear spring water, hearths and fireplaces with chimneys cut often at an angle and built of brick.

The fifties are in some ways a remote age of food rationing and housing shortages, and it is highly probable that the Kinver rock-dwellers were no worse off than many of their contemporaries in the village below. The rock bulges out from the hillside and offered commodious living space, with the addition of doors and windows as required, making the living quarters cool in hot weather, and dry in wet weather. The visitor will notice, although time and vandalism have taken their toll, the traces of lime wash and plaster on the walls, and the holes cut in the rock face for the support of roof gables and joists, for some of the dwellings had two floors. They also had neat gardens, the soil being carried up to the site.

The cave-dwellings of Holy Austin Rock were perhaps overcrowded and lacking in modern sanitation, but there is fair evidence from local burial records of continuous occupation, often by members of the same families, since 1814, and it is almost certain that the cave-dwellings were used long before that date. Most of the males were either farm labourers or worked in the local iron works until these were closed in the late 1860s. The Rock and its inhabitants feature in many old photographs and postcards made about the turn of the century, and still to be seen on the sandstone face are the words 'ROCK HOUSE CAFE', testimony to the profit to be made from curious tourists. The cafe finally closed in 1967.

(2) The plaque set in the boulder commemorates the Lee family who presented 200 acres of land adjacent to the Kingsford Country Park to the National Trust, thus enlarging this fine recreational area still further. The obelisk is a war memorial. The district is indeed fortunate in its beautiful surroundings and in the gifts of its benefactors.

SEVEN SPRINGS, CANNOCK CHASE – STEPPING STONES – SEVEN SPRINGS.

Distance 5 miles.
O.S. Maps Nos. 127 (Stafford and Telford) and 128 (Derby and Burton-on-Trent), 1:50,000.
Start point Seven Springs car park. Grid ref. 004206 on sheet No. 128.

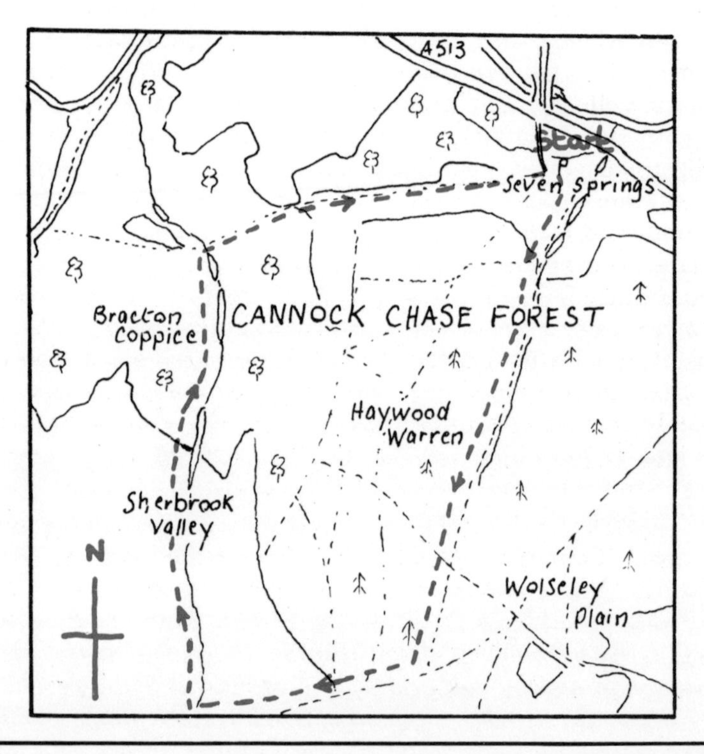

This undulating walk along firm tracks begins among the birches and bird-song of Seven Springs. From the ample car park take the track going left up the slope past some pools. It is a steady climb among the bracken and sycamore trees. Presently, as the well-made path gains height, these are replaced by tall stands of conifers – larch and spruce predominating. A rivulet trickles among the trees on the left, the water running clear over the gravelly bottom. Cuckoos and warblers abound here in summer. Here and there a stately oak appears, a survivor of the ancient forest. The topsoil is thin with layers of sand and gravel beneath it.

The track goes straight ahead and up through more bracken-covered slopes into open country cleared of trees and heather. It mounts to a T-junction. Go right and past a path coming in from the left. Here are young birch and beech trees, a welcome change from the sombre, if stately softwood trees. Proceed straight on to reach a trig. point — there is a fine view over the Chase here — and then go along the edge of the wood on the left, gradually descending down a stony track, clearly at times a water-course. Follow the edge of the wood left and down to another junction of tracks. Go right across a stream past some willows to a post, then right again down a valley which is open on both sides. This was probably once a wide river bed, and now supports heather, bilberry and bracken. The darker evergreen cowberry with its tight clusters of whitish-pink bell flowers, shows itself here and there. The cowberry hybridises with the bilberry and produces edible red berries in the autumn. This is typical heath vegetation, and soon young bedstraw and delicate yellow, four-petalled tormentils also appear.

The path swings left and then right round a boggy area, then goes downhill to an open picnic site by the water. A signpost indicates 'Stepping Stones 1 mile', and there follows a gradual descent through birch woods and past some towering ancient oaks. Turn right and cross the clear stream by the stepping stones. Notice the large, rounded pebbles hereabouts. Through forest glades, the track now leads past a grove of birch trees devastated by the parasitic fungus called Jew's ear. Each tree, gaunt and leafless, bears the symbol of its doom. The silver birch clearly likes these sandy soils, but tends to be sickly and short-lived. Fortunately it regenerates itself quickly. Soon we arrive back at Seven Springs and in the car return to the road, turn right and make for the Wolseley Arms one mile away on the Trentside. Excellent food and drink are to be had here.

The name 'Cannock' probably derives from the Celtic 'Cnoc', which meant a hilly place, and today Cannock Chase is a delightful 28 square miles of hill and vale, forest and heath on the very edge of the Black Country. It was a hunting ground for Mercian kings more than a thousand years ago, and by the time of the Domesday Survey, 1086, which claimed it for the Norman king, Cannock Chase included much of what is today Lichfield and Wolverhampton. In 1281, Edward I ordered the hunting down of all wolves in the Chase, and in 1290 the area was given to the Bishop of Lichfield. At the dissolution of the monasteries in the 16th century, Cannock Chase was awarded to the Paget family, the ancestors of the Marquis of Angelsey.

There are still herds of fallow deer in the Chase. These beautiful, shy creatures were introduced into England by the Romans, who brought them originally from Macedonia. Those now remaining in the Chase are descended from deer that escaped the 19th century huntsmen.

Much of the area was cleared for sheep pastures in the 16th and 17th centuries and later, in the 18th century, large areas of the ancient forest were cleared to provide charcoal for the iron industry before the general introduction of coke as a reducing fuel. Some of the trees of the ancient forest, largely oaks, have survived however in Brocton Coppice, which is also the favourite region of the deer. The antipodean wallaby has also colonised part of the Chase, which is astonishingly peaceful and relatively unfrequented, considering the proximity of so many industries and centres of population. The quiet of the deep woods is obviously relished by the badgers whose presence has been immortalised in the place names of Brocton Coppice and Broc Hill. The tree-lined banks of the Sherbrook are the haunts of great-tits and their lesser cousins the blue-tits and coal-tits. During the Great War the area was a vast military camp, and today contains war cemetaries for the dead of both sides, including the graves of many New Zealanders who fell victim to the Spanish influenza epidemic of 1918.

There have always been rich deposits of iron ore, lime, coal and fire clay within easy reach of the surface in this region, and the southern part of Cannock Chase has been mined since the 14th century, when pack-horses carried coal and iron to the forges. With the coming of the canals and railways, the whole region of the Black Country enjoyed a meteroic rise in economic importance, and the extraction of minerals proceeded apace, side by side with the manufacture of iron and steel. The skyline was continually lit by the glare from the blast furnaces and foundries, and the region developed its famous individual character and traditions which now, in an era of re-planning, are kept alive in the Black Country Museum at Dudley.

Famous military and naval families are also closely associated with the district. Nearby Shugborough Hall was the home of Admiral Anson who was active in 1743 in operations against Spanish ships plying the gold trade from South America, and in his ship 'Centurion' completed a circumnavigation of the globe in 1744-5. His home is now being developed as the Staffordshire Museum. The Wolseley Arms and Wolseley Park are named after Sir Garnet Wolseley, who defeated the Zulus led by Chief Cetewayo in 1879, suppressed a dangerous rebellion in Egypt in 1882, and commanded the forces which were sent too late to save General Gordon at Khartoum in 1885 – all incidents illustrating the high-water mark of Victorian imperialism.

The Paget family have always maintained close links with Cannock Chase and the title Marquess of Anglesey was granted to one of their number, second-in-command at the Battle of Waterloo, for his gallantry in the battle during which he lost a leg, an incident which occasioned probably the most laconic observation ever made on such a terrible wound: "Gad, Paget", said the Duke of Wellington, "You've lost a leg!". "By Gad, Sir", replied Paget, "So I have!". The sixth Marquess sold the southern part of the Chase to the Forestry Commission, and the rest is leased from the Earl of Lichfield. On all, both local people and visitors alike, Cannock Chase has continued to exert the same kind of quiet charm as it did on those early kings and nobles, who found there a respite from their daily worries and cares – a service it still performs for us today.

WALK 20

GORSTY HILL – ABBOTS BROMLEY – GORSTY HILL

Distance, a.m. 4 miles, p.m. approximately 4 miles.
O.S. Map No. 128 (Derby and Burton-upon-Trent), 1:50,000.
Start point and car park – the green opposite the former Wesleyan chapel, Gorsty Hill. Grid reference 100290

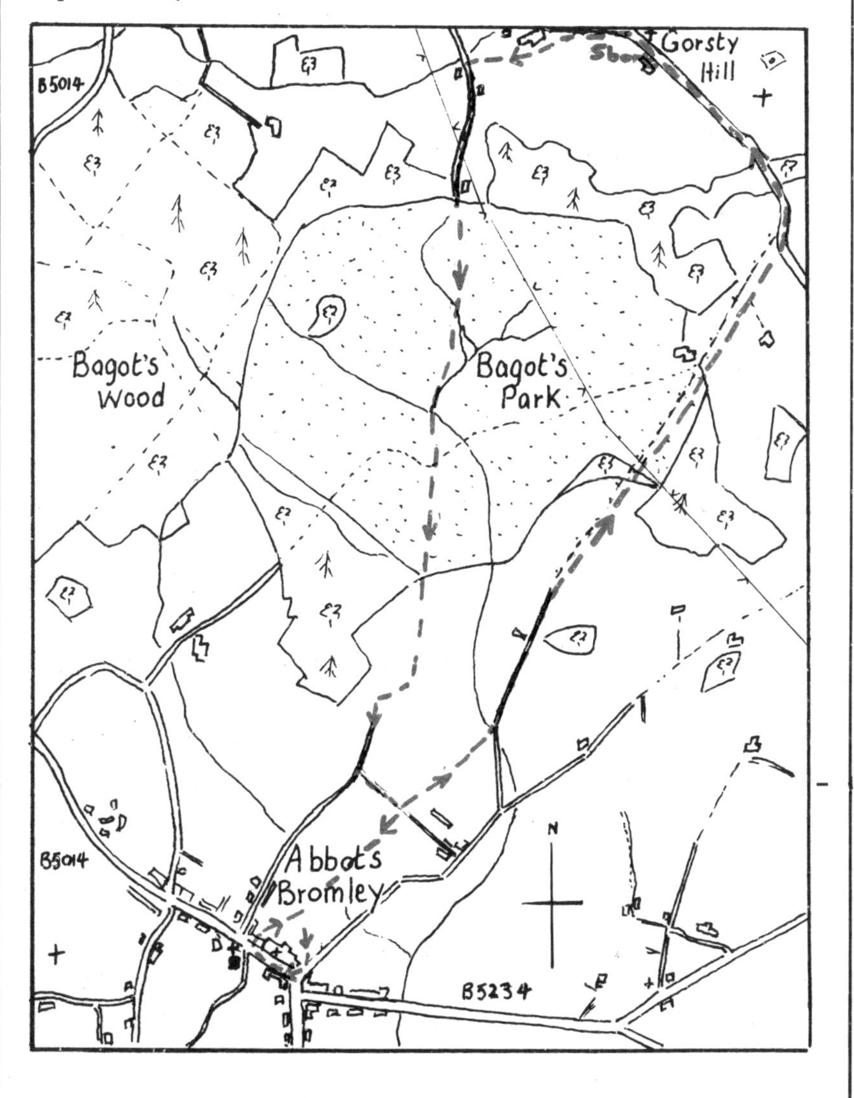

Staffordshire is a county much maligned in popular imagination, for man has imposed on it a sad dichotomy of character. To the north he has created the sprawling conurbation of the Potteries, to the south he has tortured the earth into great areas of dereliction, and to the east he has erected the odorous breweries of Burton-upon-Trent, in his remorseless quest to exploit economic wealth. The region is rich in custom and tradition, but is hardly famed for natural beauty, yet hard by, in the angle formed by Uttoxeter, Stafford and Rugeley, are the remains of the vast Needwood Forest, beloved of early kings, and still the home of tall, majestic oaks.

Here today are quiet villages watered by brooks flowing into the gentle Blithe, which in turn feeds a huge reservoir. This is beef and dairy country, the quiet Vale of Old Father Trent, the most parochial of all Midland rivers. Near Abbots Bromley (1), once a thriving market town, but now a peaceful village, by-passed by time, stands Blithfield Hall (2), home of the Bagots since the 14th century, on the banks of the reservoir which bears its name. Not far away is the fine Anglo-Catholic church of Hoar Cross (3), an experience not to be missed by the visitor to this area.

Blithe indeed is the scene of green pastures around the old chapel which is the ramble's start point. Our route is to be level, over meadow and track, with firm footing all the way. Go along the Abbots Bromley road for about 200 yards, then turn left up the lane to Knypersley Hall, taking the track on the right by a corrugated barn, alongside white railings, and in front of the black and white house. Across the yard is a red-brick barn near a gate admitting to a pasture. On the left is a quiet valley, ahead a hedgerow and a pond. Make for the stile in the right-hand corner by another pond on the left, skirt the arable field to arrive at a farm road by a black metal gate and a step-stile bearing the insignia of the Staffordshire knot to mark the Staffordshire Way.

Go down the drive away from the house to another gate and stile. Keep going along a hard track through more gates and stiles under power lines. The road is now metalled and there is another pond on the left. The pastoral scene has old-fashioned rural views with a thick wood on the right. The track goes left to a farm but our way goes straight on over another step-stile to an ancient hummocky field, which is part of Bagot's Park. The path rises to the left-hand corner by a fir coppice. Behind is a belt of mixed woodland, ahead the arable begins, and the route goes straight on keeping a wire fence on the right, to reach a copse on the left, an oasis in the ploughed land. The reason – pheasants! – dozens of them – tame and trusting. There is now a line of tall oaks, and at the end of the copse, the sign-posted way goes over a step-stile and alongside a ditch and hedge on the left.

The ditch contains Story Brook. Continue alongside this through a long field to a white metal gate and a concrete road. Go straight over and down the left-hand side of the next field, with the hedge on the left, and swing right at the bottom corner under the power lines, following another brook to a step-stile into a copse. Go through this, and uphill to a point half way along the next field, where a stile on the left admits to another field on that side. Follow the hedgerow keeping it on the right, into the corner, then follow it left under a tall oak, looking for a sign-post and stile after about 200 yards. Cross into the next field and go up alongside the right hedge. By a small oak is another sign-post and stile – go over it and then turn left up to a stile by a gate.

Follow the track beneath the trees, which soon becomes firm and acquires a name – Hadfield Lane. The lane joins a metalled road where the way goes left until a green sign for Abbots Bromley appears on the right, after half a mile. Now follow the indicated route over meadows, down a valley, over a footbridge and up the hill, finally turning left along a track past a large red-brick house on the right. Then turn right up Radmore Road to come upon the main Lichfield Road, turn right again and walk along the village street, past the girls' school, to the market place, where there is a choice of inns. The Goats Head is excellent.

After lunch, go up Schoolhouse Lane on the left of the market place, past the new Richard Clarke Primary School, as far as the old school buildings. Here, turn right up Swan Lane and right again at the end, then immediately left alongside St. Mary's and St. Anne's playing fields. Now go half left through the meadow to a gate-gap and the footbridge which was crossed in the morning. Now follow the morning route in reverse, up the slope to the top, then turn left along the green lane to the metalled road. There are fine views behind, over Rugeley power station to Cannock Chase. Cross the road and go up the drive to Radmore Farm, but where the drive swings right, go straight on over the step-stile on the left, and down the pasture, with a wire fence on the right. At the facing stile, go sharp right as indicated, and keeping the hedge on the right, cross the field to a lane. Here, turn left and walk up the gentle rise past Silverhill Stud or Moors Farm.

A rougher track takes over, goes uphill and then down to a gate and a cattle grid. There is a notice indicating 'Private Road', and the farmer assured us that the way led just inside the hedge in the field on the right. Follow this hedge through two sheep gates, and leaving the black and white farm on the left, continue to a copse, again keeping the hedge on the left. In the copse go half right and emerge in a cultivated field under crackling power lines. Now go left up the side of the field and continue on this heading, with a ditch on the right, to a metal gate with Park Lodge Farm beyond it. Turn right down the concrete road and follow the lane ahead between the wire fences. It dips down to a cattle grid, then continues with a wood and a pasture on the left, past a junction of tracks to a road. Go left up the road which descends between woods, then rises gently up past Glasshouse Farm to Gorsty Hill, giving pleasing views of the wooded ridge behind.

(1) Abbots Bromley is still a meeting place of roads from Burton-upon-Trent and Uttoxeter, though now it is far outstripped by them in importance. 'Bromley' probably means a meadow of oat-like grass, and, as was often the case in manorial times, 'Abbots' denoted the property of the church, almost certainly the Abbey of Burton, whilst its neighbour, 'King's' Bromley belonged to the crown. Its small market place, evocative of past glories, has a 17th century covered butter-market, hexagonal, and supported on pillars of stout local timber. There are still some old half-timbered houses in the village, and a row of very fine almshouses owes its origin to the Bagot family, whose influence is still very much present in the names of the two inns. The grandest building in the village is the well-known girls' public school of St. Mary and St. Anne.

In the spacious church, much restored but with traces of classical elegance – especially in the tower – are kept the reindeer horns used in the famous Horn Dance, whose origins are shrouded in mystery. The pagan ritual probably refers to the ancient forestry rites held by the early villagers, hard won and vitally important, the maintenance of which was essential to their economy. The Dance is conducted every year on the Monday after the first Sunday after the first day of September, by twelve dancers, six of whom wear the heavy, branching antlers, while there are two musicians, a Robin Hood on a hobby horse, a Maid Marian, a symbol of fertility, a jester, and a boy with a bow and arrow. They are all attired in colourful rustic costume, and perform the dance, which no doubt is also a symbolic prayer for the increase of the deer herds, all around the parish and in the grounds of Blithfield Hall, completing an exhausting day by laying up their horns again for safe keeping in the holy place until next year's wake comes round.

(2) Just off the B5013, the Uttoxeter road, is Bagot's Bromley, where a monument marks the site of the Bagot's original home. From here, in the 14th century, Ralph Bromley travelled the two miles to marry the heiress of Blithfield Hall, and founded a dynasty which has endured there ever since. This marriage produced a son, John, who built a new house of local timber, which was destined to fall into ruin through bad workmanship. He it was who added a goat's head to the family crest after receiving a herd of goats from Richard II, in gratitude for good hunting in Bagot's Park. His brother 'Bushy' Bagot features in Shakespeare's play 'Richard II', and of course in history, as Richard's evil genius.

Later there was a marriage alliance with the Staffords, Dukes of Buckingham, which might well have proved disastrous when that family's fortunes collapsed in ruin. In Elizabeth's reign, Richard Bagot, as Deputy Lieutenant of Staffordshire, had responsibility for supervising Mary Queen of Scots during her imprisonment at Tutbury and Chartley castles. Apparently he performed the role well, for the Bagots were ennobled by Elizabeth. They had strong royalist sympathies in the Civil War, and another Richard Bagot, later to be killed at Naseby, vigorously defended Lichfield for the king. Today one of their proudest possessions is a crimson satin cap, with gold and silver embroidery, once worn by Charles I.

In the 18th century Bagots were bishops of the church and diplomats, but whatever their achievements, they were fired with the same love of their ancestral home, set in the Blythe valley amid its splendid trees. The house has undergone numerous changes since the days when it was a moated Elizabethan manor, and though it was sold to the South Staffordshire Water Board when the Blithfield reservoir was first envisaged, there was a change of heart on the part of the sixth Baron and his wife, who were so moved by the thought of losing the family home forever, that they bought it back, refurbished it, and opened it to the public. The house must have been equally dear to the generations of Bagots whose tombs lie in the quiet church nearby, prominent among them being that of Sir Lewis Bagot of Tudor times, with his two wives and his nineteen children.

(3) The church of the Holy Angels, Hoar Cross, is a monument to the memory of Hugo Francis Meynell Ingram of Hoar Cross Hall, erected by his young widow, Emily Charlotte, the eldest daughter of the first Viscount Halifax.

Ingram died in 1871 after a marriage of only seven years, and it was not until thirty-three years later that his grieving widow followed him to the tomb. The whole church, built and furnished in the highest traditions of the Anglo-Catholic faith, is a shrine to the memory of the man who was descended from the father of foxhunting and the woman, devout and childless, who lies beside him in the chantry chapel. The best architects and craftsmen of the day worked with the choicest of materials – marble, sandstone, stained glass - for fourteen years, to complete this masterpiece, which was begun in 1872, opened for worship in 1876, but not finally perfected until 1906.

INDEX